PIPES

Series editor: Frédérique Crestin-Billet
Design: Lélie Carnot
Typesetting by Special Edition Pre-press Services
Translated from the French by Chet Wiener and Stacy Doris
Copy-edited by Christine Schultz-Touge
Originally published as La Folie des Pipes
© 2001 Flammarion, Paris
This English-language edition © 2002 Flammarion Inc.

ISBN: 2-0801-0884-0
Printed in France

Collectible
PIPES

Jean Rebeyrolles

Flammarion

This smiling face greeted me with my first "mature" purchase, back when I was still spending my small allowance on toy soldiers and matchbox cars. The handsome blue wrapper on the Amsterdamer fijne snede gave off an intoxicating scent and I hurried home to give the tobacco a try. Thanks to a pipe I had salvaged and matches swiped from an unsuspecting uncle, I lit up and entered what I considered the "grown-up world." The grown-ups I was thinking about were great ship captains, detectives, and writers such as Sir Walter Raleigh, Sherlock Holmes, and Ernest Hemmingway!

CONTENTS

Introduction

Henri-Louis Duhamel du Monceau described the ubiquity of smoking throughout the world in *The Art of Pipe Making* (1777). "The use of inhaling smoke from burning plants is an extensive practice, not only among established nations, but everywhere." Smoke had been used to preserve food, to ward off insects, in the tracking of animals, in sacrifices, religious ceremonies, and for medicinal purposes. While tobacco has been smoked in North and South America and the Caribbean since prehistoric times, the first Europeans to encounter it were Christopher Columbus and his crew, in the 1490s. When Edmund Spenser mentioned "divine Tobacco" in the *Fairie Queene* in 1590, people were just beginning to smoke for pleasure in Europe. Before that, if high society knew of smoking at all, it was as a cure for various ailments. Not until the time of Sir Walter Raleigh with his influence on Queen Elizabeth and her court did pipe smoking take off. Pipe size, materials, and design have been evolving ever since.

W hile humans have been smoking for about as long as they have known how to use fire, evidence indicates that aromatic plants such as hemp and certain creeping vines, thought to have magical powers, were initially smoked in rituals or used as aphrodisiacs.

The first trace of pipes can be seen on bas-reliefs, while archeological digs have uncovered iron Celtic pipes, as well as clay pipes throughout Europe dating from Roman times—even though tobacco was then unknown on the continent. Such pipes were unearthed in Holland, England, Italy, and Spain. Danish pipes have been found in Ireland, tiny *piob shith*, fairy or elfin pipes, have turned up in Scotland, copper and brass pipes have been discovered in Africa, and silver and stone pipes have appeared in Asia.

There are few traces of pipe smoking during the Middle Ages in the Western world. It seems that the practice, which had been fairly widespread a few centuries earlier, was nearly

Aztec stone pipe.
Three people could
smoke simultaneously.

abandoned. Still some evidence does exist. For example, in his book *La Pipe* (1973), the historian Paul Bastien documented sculpted ornaments on an eleventh-century church in Huberville, France, as well as on a striking thirteenth-century tomb in western Ireland. The Irish tomb is in the Abbey of Burren in Corcomroe. A life-size effigy represents Siudaine O'Brian, Lord of Thommond; he holds a pipe in his left hand.

Dating early clay pipes discovered in archeological digs is often quite difficult. Does this one predate the arrival of tobacco in Europe?

Is this an incense burner or a pipe? Experts continue to debate whether humans or gods were the intended recipients of this artifact's smoke, and whether it was even used for tobacco. Found in Mexico, the decoration is a completely nude man.

The peoples of Central America, Mexico, Brazil, Cuba, and several Caribbean islands were smoking tobacco when the first Europeans arrived. Columbus's crew encountered the indigenous people of Cuba smoking "rolled cones of burning leaves." Later in their travels, the sailors came upon the Arawaks of Haiti smoking what they called "tobacco" in their native language. When French explorers and missionaries arrived in Brazil, they were told that the plant had healing properties.

Yet it was Spanish and Portuguese sailors that first introduced tobacco smoking to landlubbers. English sailors, for their part, were instrumental in introducing it to other seamen, particularly Russians.

A tobacco plant in flower.

The scene is not difficult to imagine. A Spanish sailor arrives in a French harbor. He sidles up to a table at a portside inn or tavern, takes a clay pipe out of his pocket, and pinches out some of the strange brownish leaves between two callused fingers. Then, slowly and carefully, he strikes a match and sets light to the mixture in the bowl of the pipe, drawing in air from the other end. The room fills with the unfamiliar scent, and everyone is filled with curiosity about this strange aromatic smoke. Amid animated conversation, the pipe makes its way around the room for everyone to try in turn. And thus the practice continued to spread from port to port, and thence to towns and cities inland throughout Europe.

Pipe tobacco. Quality and flavor have evolved tremendously over the centuries.

INTRODUCTION

Although André Thevet, a French Franciscan monk, first brought tobacco plants to Europe from Brazil in the 1550s, the consumption of tobacco did not begin there until around 1560. A decisive step was taken by Jean Nicot (1530–1600), after whom nicotine was named. As the French ambassador to Portugal, he procured some tobacco for Catherine de' Medici, then queen of France, hoping that it might help relieve her famous migraine headaches. The queen's delight with tobacco led to a more widespread interest for smoking in France and Jean Nicot soon became famous. This led to complaints from André Thevet who was angered that Nicot, who had never set foot in Brazil, had given his name to the monk's discovery.

At about the same time in England, the ladies of Queen Elizabeth I's court took to smoking pipes in honor of her favorite, Sir Walter Raleigh. This great navigator had, during his many travels, encountered the practice in Virginia and is credited with having introduced potatoes and tobacco into Britain. The practice of smoking quickly gained popularity on both sides of the Channel. Such was its success that King Louis XIII forbade the sale of tobacco in France and Pope Urban VIII even took the step of excommunicating smokers.

Gentleman smoking a Dutch pipe. Despite contemporary efforts to prohibit the practice, scenes like this one became more and more common.

Sir Walter Raleigh (left) was an intrepid sea captain, writer, politician and trendsetter. He organized colonizing expeditions to America and privateering expeditions against Spanish and Portuguese ships. With Raleigh's personality behind the practice, tobacco smoking's popularity spread tremendously. Pipe-smoking clubs appeared throughout England—women and even children were avid smokers.

But the atmosphere changed in England when King James succeeded to the throne. Pushed by anti-tobacco interests and parties friendly to Spain, the new king had Raleigh executed in 1618. Legend has it that his last act, as he climbed the scaffold, was smoking a pipe.

Meanwhile, Catholics and some Protestant groups fled England to escape mounting persecution. In 1617 one such enterprising émigré, William Baernelts set off for Holland, settling in Gouda, which was known for its pottery. He changed his name to the native-sounding Willem Barentz and founded Europe's first clay pipe factory, choosing the Tudor rose for his trademark. Many others followed his example, and soon clay pipes were being manufactured in Belgium, then in Normandy, Brittany, and the south of France.

While today the mention of the word pipe may immediately call to mind a finely crafted briarwood object with a black stem, in eighteenth-century Europe the term "pipe" could be applied to any item made of clay.

Native Americans used stone pipes or Y-shaped hose-inhaling pipes, and the first tobacco pipes brought from North America to Europe had very small clay bowls with wood stems. Most of the first clay pipes imported to the American colonies were Dutch-made, although English pipes soon reached the shores. Native Americans continued to make

Traditional Dutch-style clay pipes. After being produced in Holland, pipes like these were manufactured throughout Europe and then the rest of the world.

a small number of pipes, and others were made locally using imported molds.

The Dixon Company of Montreal was one of the first important North American pipe makers. Northern Europe and Scandinavia produced a good number of clay pipes, as did Scotland, as represented by McDougall and Burton. We will also see many excellent examples from Fiolet and Gambier, two large-scale French producers, established in the seventeenth century, and Dutel-Giscoln, Blanc-Garin, and Duméril-Leurs, which were founded in the eighteenth century. Thousands of pipes were produced daily, but due to their fragility only a tiny fraction have survived to this day. Yet they do appear regularly in special sales, collector's forums, and antique stores.

Left: pipe case, complete with tobacco stash. Facing page: The diversity of clay pipe models is immense—as you will discover in subsequent pages.

While in France, England, and North America clay pipes were smoked, Germany began working in porcelain. Hard-paste porcelain was first successfully devised in Saxony in 1709, and within about a quarter of a century the process was transferred to the manufacture of porcelain pipes. Advances in both quality and form followed apace. While it is still breakable, porcelain is more durable than clay, but it is also less porous, and therefore the quality of the smoke is not as good. On the other hand, the number of variations in design and color that are possible on porcelain make for a treasure trove of possibilities for the modern-day collector.

In addition to being attractive porcelain pipes are often very practical. Many are comprised of two

Porcelain pipes from Germany. Porcelain pipes were often painted by hand and usually depicted hunting, village, or agricultural scenes. Sometimes kitsch or quaint themes become just a tad saucy.

pieces: the bowl and the socket. This offers two surfaces for decorating, while the design of the socket allows for collection of both saliva and the moisture released when lighting up. The ease with which these pipes can be taken apart facilitates cleaning—a necessity due to the material's lack of porosity.

Austria, Switzerland, and Czechoslovakia became major porcelain pipe-producing nations. Parts of the United States soon followed as immigrants from these countries settled and continued the tradition.

Left: Before briarwood's merits were discovered, boxwood and other kinds of wood were used internationally during the same period that porcelain pipes were popular in Central and Eastern Europe.

A porcelain pipe with all its original parts. This image provides a good indication of typical size.

Meerschaum soon overtook porcelain for the ideal pipe. Meerschaum, which means "sea foam" in German, is so light that it floats on water. This mineral composed of hydrous magnesium silicate is relatively rare, and is found primarily off the coast of Turkey, although "deposits" can be found in Crimea and off the Greek island of Negrepont, as well as in small quantities elsewhere.

Legend has it that the vogue for meerschaum pipes was started after the Hungarian Count Andrassy returned from Turkey in the eighteenth century and handed a piece over to his cobbler

A catalogue page from Sommer's of Paris. While meerschaum artists carved this excellent material into many original designs, classic forms were nevertheless represented.

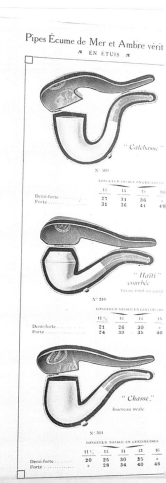

– **26** –

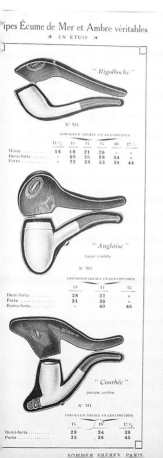

ipes Écume de Mer et Ambre véritables
EN ÉTUIS

" Rigolboche "

N° 512

LONGUEUR TOTALE EN CENTIMÈTRES

	11½	13	14	15	16	17½
Mince	14	18	21	26	»	»
Demi-forte	»	20	25	29	34	»
Forte	»	23	28	33	38	44

" Anglaise "
foyer mobile

N° 513

LONGUEUR TOTALE EN CENTIMÈTRES

	13	14	15
Demi-forte	28	32	»
Forte	31	36	»
Extra-forte	»	40	45

" Courbée "
pompe ambre

N° 514

LONGUEUR TOTALE EN CENTIMÈTRES

	15	16	17½
Demi-forte	29	34	39
Forte	33	38	45

SOMMER FRÈRES PARIS

asking that he sculpt it into a pipe. The cobbler complied, shaping the meerschaum like a typical wooden pipe of the time. Andrassy was a highly visible public figure, and when he sported his meerschaum pipe about town, it caught on like wildfire.

Before this point, meerschaum had been used to filter perfumes in Turkey, and the Turks may have first realized that it was a fine filter for tobacco too. The great population fluxes, within the Austro-Hungarian empire during the eighteenth century, seem to have contributed in the use of meerschaum further north.

Meerschaum pipes have been made throughout eastern Europe, but the undeniable meerschaum capital is Vienna, where a sort of second-grade meerschaum was also invented. This

Meerschaum pipes are made almost exclusively in Turkey, where the material is primarily found. That country has prohibited the export of meerschaum in its raw form (see page 215).

material is composed of small fragments of meerschaum combined with fatty matter. The resulting mixture is then molded into shape. Known as Vienna meerschaum, it closely resembles the real thing and enables intricate sculpting.

Authentic meerschaum can be finely carved because it takes on a consistency similar to chalk when wet. It is traditionally treated with beeswax or sperm whale ointment, known as spermaceti. The enticing seasoned look on old, well-used meerschaum results from the smoking process itself. Burning tobacco causes the spermaceti coating to melt and forces it towards the meerschaum's surface. Meanwhile, as it melts it combines with the tobacco's tar. When the pipe cools the tars remain on the surface and the ointment or beeswax reverts back towards the interior. Because there is an inverse relation between density and temperature the chamber area usually remains white while the further reaches become richer and deeper in colour. The best meerschaum artists are able to take full advantage of this natural effect, knowing that over time sculpted faces will remain light in hue while the beard and hair around them will take on darker, burnished tones. The pipes featured pages 137 and 160 illustrate this darkening process.

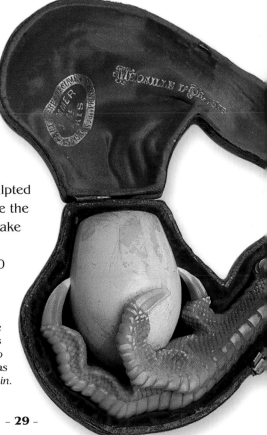

A vintage meerschaum pipe. Note the excellent seasoning. In the early stages of seasoning care must be taken not to touch the material with bare hands, as finger marks will remain.

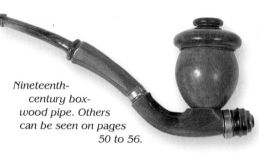

Nineteenth-century box-wood pipe. Others can be seen on pages 50 to 56.

With ancestors both prestigious and simple, briarwood is the acknowledged prince of the pipe world. It has numerous advantages over other materials. In addition to its excellent porosity, it is much less fragile than clay, porcelain, and meerschaum. Being a wood, it of course burns, although extremely slowly. The taste which burning briar conferred on the relatively poor quality tobacco of early days was greatly appreciated.

How and when the excellent qualities of briarwood were discovered remains an open question. Was it a shepherd who hit upon them, carving a bramble to pass the time during cold winter nights? Some give credit to woodworkers in the village of Cogolin, near Saint Tropez, where briar pipes are still being made today. The village of Saint-Claude in the Jura region of eastern France gets credit for the first large-scale makers of

View of Saint-Claude, one of the pipe-making capitals of the world. Two rivers, the Tacon and the Bienne converge here. Their harnessed energy proved instrumental in the development of the town's nineteenth-century industries.

But. Gilbron, Cartes postt. Saint-Claude

briarwood pipes in the early nineteenth century. The village, which remains one of the most important pipe-making centers in the world, was followed by regions of Italy, Denmark, Ireland and elsewhere. A merchant of turned wood from the Jura was visiting Napoleon's birthplace in Corsica when he broke his meerschaum pipe. He asked a local artisan to carve him a new one, and the artisan chose briarwood. The merchant immediately noticed the quality of the wood and hurried back to Saint-Claude to get things going.

Briar comes from the heath tree (*Erica arborea*). Of the four hundred species, many are native to South Africa. But the Mediterranean basin, both in Europe and Asia Minor, has a fine share. Pipes made from briarwood, also called brier, *bruyère*, French briar, and briarroot, are actually made from burls that form just above the roots. A burl must be at least thirty years old before being cut from the tree, and is sometimes much older.

An early nineteenth-century Saint-Claude workshop specializing in polishing. In many countries, polishing wood pipes and brushwork on clay pipes are traditionally done by women.

We can take the Saint-Claude method as exemplary for describing how briarwood pipes are made. After the burls are dug up and cleaned they are shipped to the town where they are sawn into the blocks called "stummels" or *ébauchons*, which will be carved into individual pipes. The blocks are sorted into quality categories and boiled in large copper cauldrons which enables the wood both to give off sap and to take on tannins, producing the dark brown color. After about a month of drying they are sorted again and sent to the factory, where slow-drying continues for months or years.

Fabrication proceeds according to the following stages, whether the briar pipe is made by machine or by hand. The first step consists in size calibration and classification. Similar *ébauchons* are hallmarked to become the same model. Then comes the rough cut (*ébauchage*), which includes the creation of the bowl and the hollowing out of two-thirds of the chamber, followed by planing (*varlopage*) when the wood is turned on a lathe and the stem is created. The base is made next, by milling

Open-work drying is usually reserved for the finest quality stummels or ébauchons. Blocks must be periodically repositioned. Lower quality briarwood is dried with the circulation of hot air in closed rooms.

(*fraisage*), and then hand-sanded. After boring of the air passage, which is one of the most touchy operations, the bowl and shank are complete. Experts then evaluate the qualitative characteristics for final determinations concerning the finishing of the pipe. If any minute flaws (called pits) are discovered they are patched with putty (a procedure that in no way inhibits the quality of smoking and should be almost imperceptible), and finally the chamber surface is polished. After this the bit or mouthpiece is mounted. Finishing operations such as dying, polishing, stamping with a model name, and so on, may then follow as well.

Most non-smoker pipe collectors are interested in older pipes.

The first two stages: from stummel to rough cut.

The next stages: planed and milled.

A fabrication diorama made by the Chacom company. If you come across one of these at a flea market don't pass it up. They are very rare.

Smokers, on the other hand have a great number of excellent new models and makes to choose from. Contemporary pipes made in the French Jura region, those made in Denmark by Sixten Ivarson or the W. Ø. Larsen family, in Germany by Rainer Barbi or Karl Heinz Joura, in Italy by Castello, in America by Paul Bonaquisti, Jody Davis, or Ron Fairchild, will certainly become the collector's items of future generations. Their quality is more than sufficient—all they lack is the mark of time.

Pipes of recent fabrication. See pages 118 to 123
for a selection of contemporary design models.

I
CLASSIC
pipes

It was Sir Walter Raleigh, Queen Elizabeth I's favorite, who made tobacco a must in the English court. Raleigh also instigated the start-up of the pipe industry, which soon expanded throughout Europe. And it was he who first asked the wonderful question: what is the weight of smoke? According to Raleigh, the answer could come from weighing tobacco before smoking it, then weighing the ashes that remained in the pipe after smoking. The difference between the two would equal the weight of smoke. This complex problem has probably never entered the heads of most pipe makers, who devote their attention to creating their own smoking wonders.

*These seventeenth-century clay pipes
(facing page) were unearthed by chance in
various archeological digs. They come from
England, France, and Holland, and are the
historic "ancestors" of everything you'll
see in this book.*

*The hunting horn is one of the great classic
Dutch pipes. It comes in a variety of sizes and
coil shapes. This one, made by Goedewaagen,
in Gouda, measures under 2 inches (5 cm).*

*This classic clay pipe is
simplicity itself, despite the
small decorative flourish
below the bowl. The
explosion of pipe
materials and designs was
about to begin.*

This long English pipe, signed Crop, measures almost 8 inches (20 cm) in length. It was made to commemorate the occasion of the London Exhibition of 1862. In England similar models, called Christmas Pipes, were hung on Christmas trees. Today, the term usually refers to a fine new briarwood collectible.

Clay pipes have gone through a variety of innovative stages and developments. This Gambier model, made for the Paris Olympics of 1900, is hand-enameled, with the letters skillfully brushed onto the round surface.

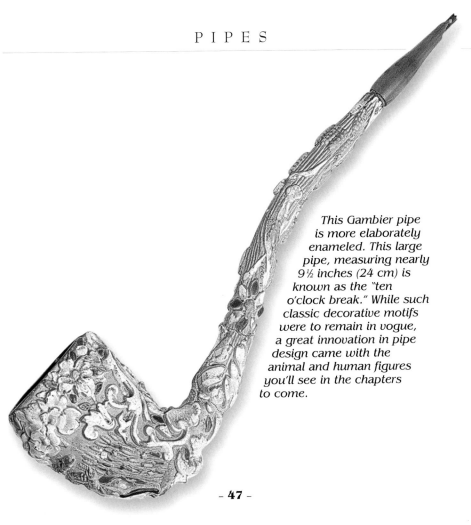

This Gambier pipe is more elaborately enameled. This large pipe, measuring nearly 9½ inches (24 cm) is known as the "ten o'clock break." While such classic decorative motifs were to remain in vogue, a great innovation in pipe design came with the animal and human figures you'll see in the chapters to come.

These two curious pipes have clay bowls. The tinted red clay bowl has a little spur. The white Gambier bowl seems to have been rarely used. In fact the bone stems on both models seem to be the result of patch-up jobs.

The rather approximate mounting and solidity support the theory that they are later attachments, replacing broken clay stems. Very suspicious.

The briar pipe was not invented until the mid-nineteenth century, so Saint-Claude pipes like this one were at first made of local boxwood. This eighteenth-century model has a metal-clad chamber and a horn stem. Note the large acorn-shaped valve.

Before becoming a capital of pipes, the French town of Saint-Claude was a center for turning all sorts of wooden objects as well as for making pipe stems—most notably from horn—for German and Austrian makers. These two specialties are clearly expressed in this model from the first half of the nineteenth century.

Like the pipes on the preceding double page, the stems of these three boxwood pipes are more extensively worked than their bowls. They are fine examples of the art of turning.

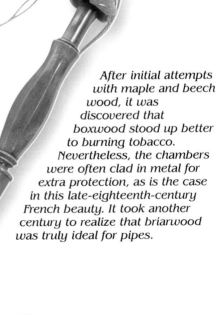

After initial attempts
with maple and beech
wood, it was
discovered that
boxwood stood up better
to burning tobacco.
Nevertheless, the chambers
were often clad in metal for
extra protection, as is the case
in this late-eighteenth-century
French beauty. It took another
century to realize that briarwood
was truly ideal for pipes.

Novelty is not everything. This early-nineteenth-century French pipe is based on an old-fashioned Dutch model. The boxwood bowl is mounted on a horn stem. The valve is also made of horn.

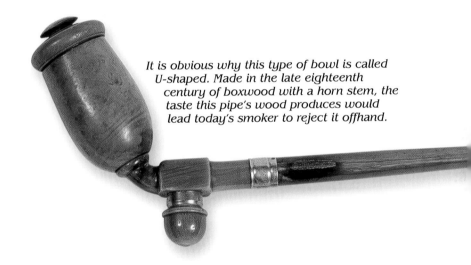

It is obvious why this type of bowl is called U-shaped. Made in the late eighteenth century of boxwood with a horn stem, the taste this pipe's wood produces would lead today's smoker to reject it offhand.

This handsome boxwood model, from the early nineteenth century, has a metal-clad chamber and a nifty lid. Its wavy bowl carving brings to mind the meerschaum pipes of the same era.

On the other hand, this darkly seasoned eighteenth-century meerschaum bowl resembles wood. Its similarity to the facing wood bowl is striking.

Meerschaum comes from Turkey (see page 26). The Turks occupied Hungary throughout the seventeenth century, and extended up as far as Vienna at two points in time. The mix of populations in the Austro-Hungarian Empire made Vienna the world's meerschaum pipe capital in the eighteenth century. This model dates from that era.

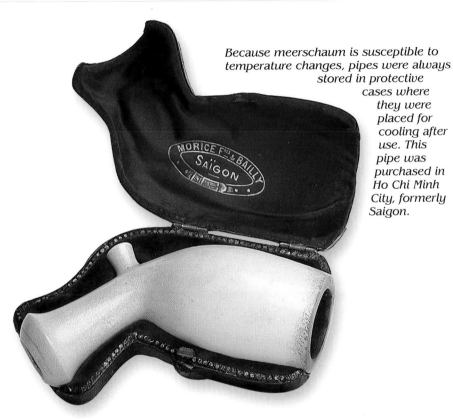

Because meerschaum is susceptible to temperature changes, pipes were always stored in protective cases where they were placed for cooling after use. This pipe was purchased in Ho Chi Minh City, formerly Saigon.

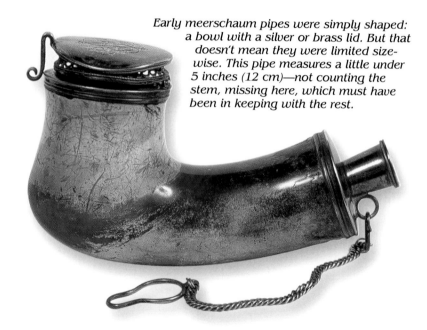

Early meerschaum pipes were simply shaped: a bowl with a silver or brass lid. But that doesn't mean they were limited size-wise. This pipe measures a little under 5 inches (12 cm)—not counting the stem, missing here, which must have been in keeping with the rest.

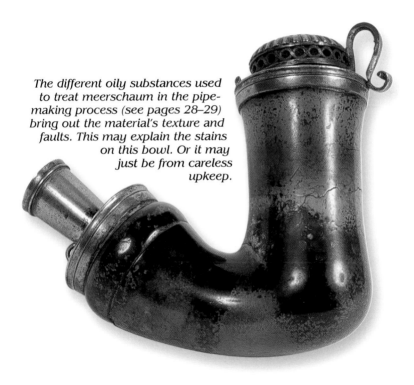

The different oily substances used to treat meerschaum in the pipe-making process (see pages 28–29) bring out the material's texture and faults. This may explain the stains on this bowl. Or it may just be from careless upkeep.

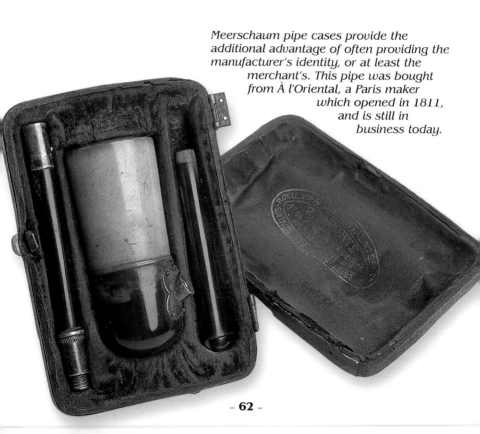

Meerschaum pipe cases provide the additional advantage of often providing the manufacturer's identity, or at least the merchant's. This pipe was bought from À l'Oriental, a Paris maker which opened in 1811, and is still in business today.

Meerschaum pipes often have amber stems. This majestic fossil resin, semi-opaque or transparent, comes in a range of colors running from pale green to red, by way of every shade of yellow. Its golden and burnished tones go perfectly with meerschaum hues.

Porcelain pipes were first made in the German province of Saxony, during the second half of the eighteenth century. Hard-paste porcelain was first made in Europe in Meissen, Germany, in 1709, where this lovely late-eighteenth-century piece was produced.

Porcelain's relative solidity made it a technological advance over clay. In addition, it makes a fine painting surface for decoration. Hunting scenes were popular on early-nineteenth-century Meissen pipes like this one.

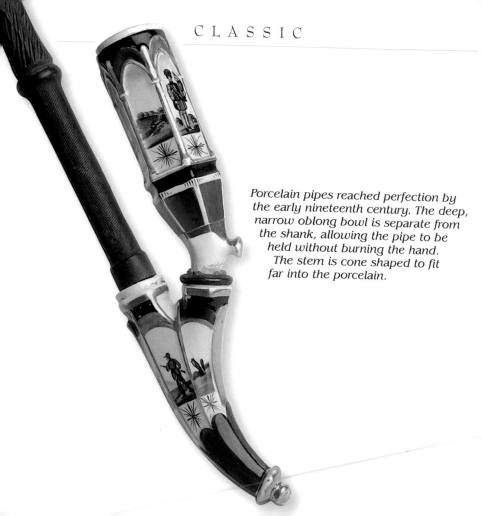

Porcelain pipes reached perfection by
the early nineteenth century. The deep,
narrow oblong bowl is separate from
the shank, allowing the pipe to be
held without burning the hand.
The stem is cone shaped to fit
far into the porcelain.

Like commemorative army
pipes, school theme pipes
were popular. This pipe was
given as a "token of
friendship" by a certain Stahl
to his classmate Schmid at
Erlangen in Bavaria, Germany.
"Let Pharmacy be Our Banner"
it reads, with a date of 1879.
The bone and wood stem is
attached with cork joints.

This little pipe is under 2 inches (5 cm), not including the stem. Aside from its decorative pompoms, the thin cord also serves to attach the bowl to the stem.

Today's pipe smokers say that porcelain can ruin the taste of even the finest tobacco blends. This nineteenth-century model can't be accused of this shortcoming. Although it is in porcelain style, it is made of glazed clay.

Porcelain pipes were a popular specialty in Germany and Czechoslovakia. They were less common in Switzerland, and only a few pricey models were ever produced in France, at the Sèvres porcelain works. This surprising pipe advertises a Belgian brand of milk skimmer, but the pipe itself was made in Germany, to spread the word to German consumers. The pipe on the facing page is more classic in style, with a handsome six-sided bowl. It was made in Meissen in the late eighteenth century.

The beauty of collecting porcelain pipes comes from the diversity of their painted decorations. The stems are another, secondary question. A weighty one, though, since they can measure more than 3 feet (1 meter). This pipe depicts "The Oath." The pipes on the facing page illustrate farming topics. The one on the left has to do with an association, but you need to be a German ace to make it out. The less wordy pipe on the right is typical of the country genre.

*This monochrome bowl displays the tools
of the baker's guild. It is mounted on a horn
shank meant to fit a horn stem. Wood or
horn? The question is one of taste
and means.*

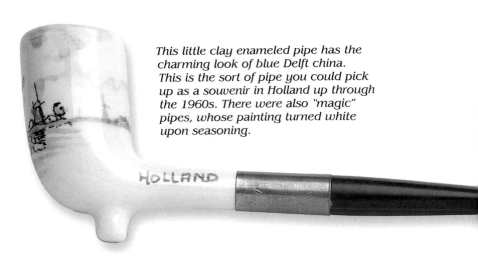

This little clay enameled pipe has the charming look of blue Delft china. This is the sort of pipe you could pick up as a souvenir in Holland up through the 1960s. There were also "magic" pipes, whose painting turned white upon seasoning.

*Pipes with curved shanks are called Bents.
Extreme models are sometimes called Hunters.
But the most curved of all are calabashes, like
these. Fresh calabash gourds may be full of
pulp and seeds but they take on the hardness
of wood with drying. This pipe's bowl is
lined with metal. The stem is amber.*

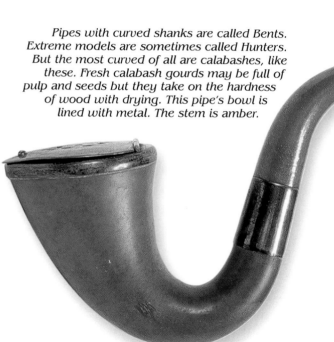

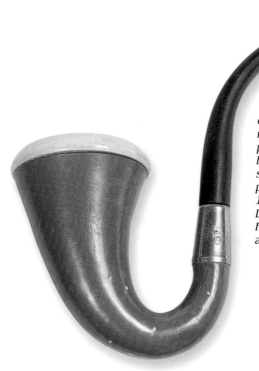

The chamber of this calabash is made of meerschaum. Calabash pipes take on a burnished beauty with seasoning. They were popular throughout the 1930s in Austria, Denmark, England, France, and the States, as well as South Africa.

After the gourd, try corn. Popularized
by General MacArthur, the corncob pipe
was invented by a Missouri farmer
around 1870. It is a marvel of simplicity.
A thoroughly dried cob of a tough strain
of corn is carved out for the head.
The chamber is sanded, and
sometimes coated in plaster or even
honey, to sweeten the smoke.
Millions of corncob pipes are still
made today. They are inexpensive
and make for nice smoking.
The only problem is they
wear out quickly, and you
need a new one every
six months or so.

This cherry wood pipe is a souvenir special, like little ceramic clogs or miniature jugs of maple syrup. It is fine for smoking, too, and the fragrant wood smells nice once the pipe has gone out.

*Cherry wood
pipes have their fans to
this day. They are still sold by
Ropp, which began making them in 1860,
in the Doubs region of France.*

This nineteenth-century briar pipe was made in Saint-Claude, France, and is faithful in form to Dutch pipes, which are said, however, to have a Belgian shape. The heel, the cylindrical protuberance at the base of the bowl, hearkens back to clay molds.

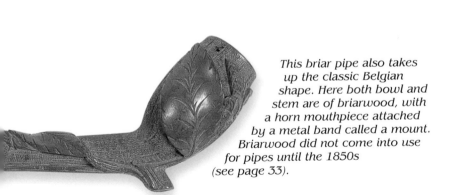

This briar pipe also takes up the classic Belgian shape. Here both bowl and stem are of briarwood, with a horn mouthpiece attached by a metal band called a mount. Briarwood did not come into use for pipes until the 1850s (see page 33).

This is a souvenir par excellence from Saint-Claude, the town in France famous for its pipes and white wine. The model dates from the 1950s. True, the carved flower is an edelweiss, which only grows in the Alps. But a sleigh-full of identical pipes marked Chamonix can explain the choice of decoration.

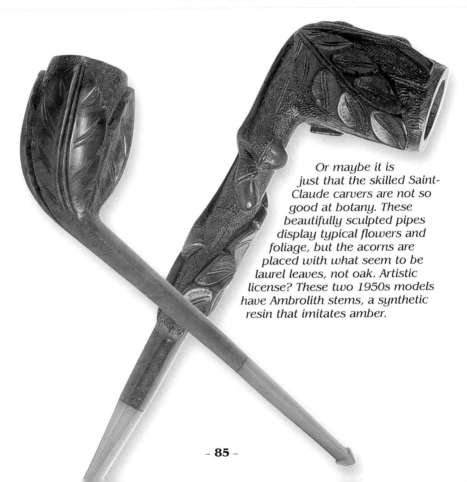

Or maybe it is just that the skilled Saint-Claude carvers are not so good at botany. These beautifully sculpted pipes display typical flowers and foliage, but the acorns are placed with what seem to be laurel leaves, not oak. Artistic license? These two 1950s models have Ambrolith stems, a synthetic resin that imitates amber.

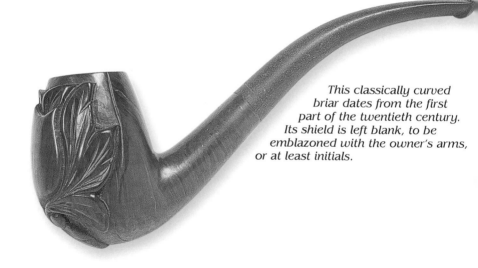

*This classically curved
briar dates from the first
part of the twentieth century.
Its shield is left blank, to be
emblazoned with the owner's arms,
or at least initials.*

There is no mistaking the vegetation on these 1950s briar pipes. No fooling around in Saint-Claude when it comes to grapes and vine leaves.

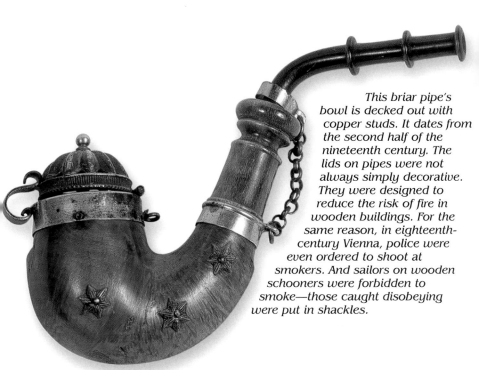

This briar pipe's bowl is decked out with copper studs. It dates from the second half of the nineteenth century. The lids on pipes were not always simply decorative. They were designed to reduce the risk of fire in wooden buildings. For the same reason, in eighteenth-century Vienna, police were even ordered to shoot at smokers. And sailors on wooden schooners were forbidden to smoke—those caught disobeying were put in shackles.

Here, the horn stem has been handsomely turned. In case of damage from chewing, the mouthpiece could be clipped to the next bit ring. Some clay pipes also had this feature.

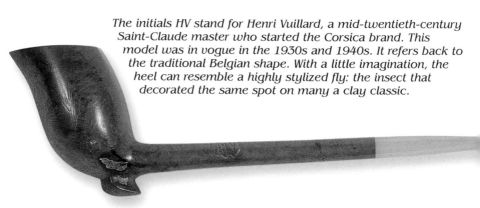

The initials HV stand for Henri Vuillard, a mid-twentieth-century
Saint-Claude master who started the Corsica brand. This
model was in vogue in the 1930s and 1940s. It refers back to
the traditional Belgian shape. With a little imagination, the
heel can resemble a highly stylized fly: the insect that
decorated the same spot on many a clay classic.

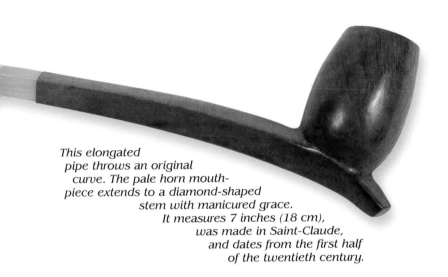

*This elongated
pipe throws an original
curve. The pale horn mouthpiece extends to a diamond-shaped
stem with manicured grace.
It measures 7 inches (18 cm),
was made in Saint-Claude,
and dates from the first half
of the twentieth century.*

Three pipes of
rare elegance grace
these two pages. Made
in the early twentieth
century, their stems have the
lofty lightness of smoke itself. This
one has an oval bowl, with a fine
security chain holding the metal
to the bone.

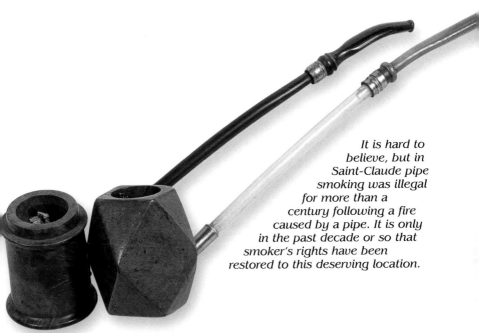

It is hard to believe, but in Saint-Claude pipe smoking was illegal for more than a century following a fire caused by a pipe. It is only in the past decade or so that smoker's rights have been restored to this deserving location.

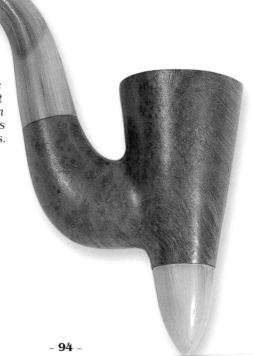

The foot and stem of this handsome model are crafted in blond horn. Towns specializing in horn-work naturally sprung up around those where pipes were made—or was it the other way around? In any case, good business makes good neighbors.

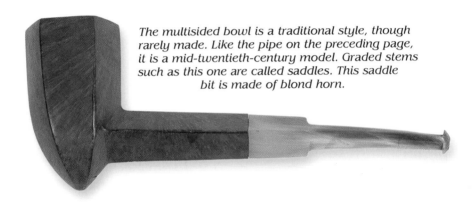

The multisided bowl is a traditional style, though rarely made. Like the pipe on the preceding page, it is a mid-twentieth-century model. Graded stems such as this one are called saddles. This saddle bit is made of blond horn.

The descriptive names for classic pipe shapes include Billiard, Freehand, Apple, Pot, Bulldog, Dublin, Canadian, and Poker. These standards are of course subject to infinite variations. This late-nineteenth-century model has a bone valve knob.

A briar pipe's value is determined by the wood's quality, grain, and beauty of its vein pattern. These two freehand pipes were fashioned by artisans who knew how to show the material at its best.

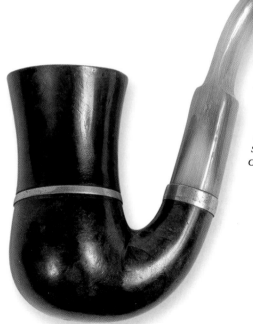

This substantial looking pipe may bring to mind German porcelain models, minus the painted decoration, of course. The briarwood has a walnut stain, a common method for covering little imperfections.

From the first half of the twentieth century, this pipe guarantees its briar authenticity with a prominent seal in gold relief letters. The somewhat flared shape seems a variant of the curved Dublin model. The stem is of contoured horn.

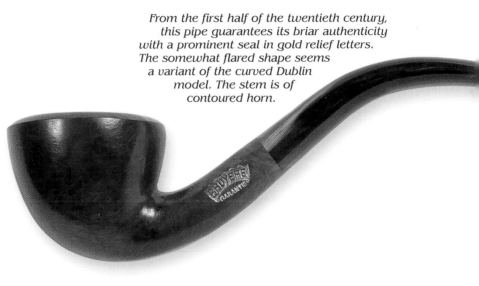

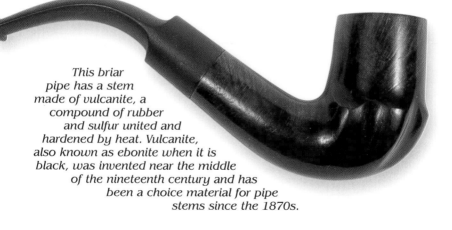

*This briar
pipe has a stem
made of vulcanite, a
compound of rubber
and sulfur united and
hardened by heat. Vulcanite,
also known as ebonite when it is
black, was invented near the middle
of the nineteenth century and has
been a choice material for pipe
stems since the 1870s.*

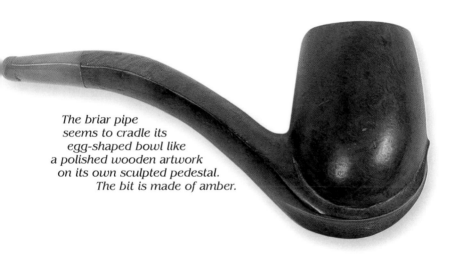

*The briar pipe
seems to cradle its
egg-shaped bowl like
a polished wooden artwork
on its own sculpted pedestal.
The bit is made of amber.*

Briar or meerschaum, that is the question. Skillful pipe makers over the years have deliberately teased the collector's eye by making one resemble the other. This meerschaum model is deeply seasoned to take on the burnished patina of wood—literally too good to be true.

On the flip side, wooden pipe masters have been known to take their cues from porcelain, meerschaum, and even calabash models, which themselves may have been inspired by clay or older forms. Such subtle overlays, differences, and correspondences all make pipe collecting so rewarding.

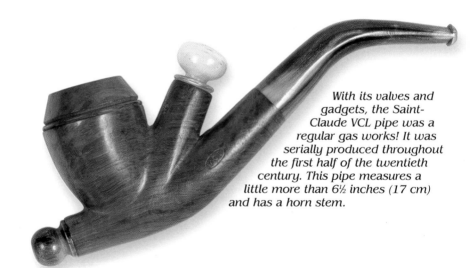

With its valves and gadgets, the Saint-Claude VCL pipe was a regular gas works! It was serially produced throughout the first half of the twentieth century. This pipe measures a little more than 6½ inches (17 cm) and has a horn stem.

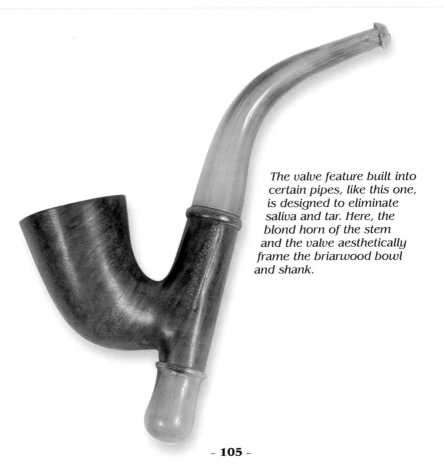

The valve feature built into certain pipes, like this one, is designed to eliminate saliva and tar. Here, the blond horn of the stem and the valve aesthetically frame the briarwood bowl and shank.

The bowl of this sandblasted briarwood pipe has a raised, pebbly finish that makes it look like lava. The stem is equally deceptive: the original albatross bone piece is replaced by a copy, and the faux-bone mouthpiece is made of acrylic.

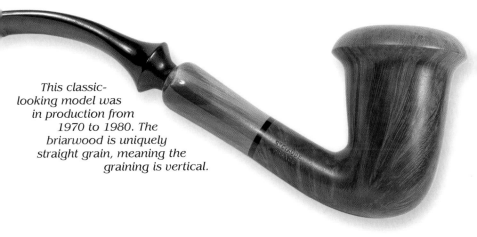

This classic-looking model was in production from 1970 to 1980. The briarwood is uniquely straight grain, meaning the graining is vertical.

A sculpturally tubby pipe, this model has the rarity of a decorated ebonite stem. While ebonite, named for its ebony color, has been used for pipe stems on a large scale since the early twentieth century, it is not commonly adorned with such faux-wood carving motifs. The stems are independently manufactured and delivered to pipe makers who contour them with heat or electric radiation.

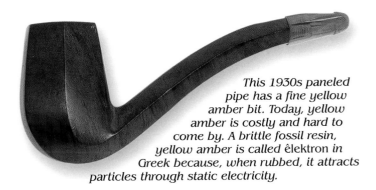

This 1930s paneled pipe has a fine yellow amber bit. Today, yellow amber is costly and hard to come by. A brittle fossil resin, yellow amber is called êlektron in Greek because, when rubbed, it attracts particles through static electricity.

This pipe's bowl is a generously flared Dublin shape. The stem is not made of horn as you might assume, but of a synthetic resin called Jubelith used throughout the 1960s.

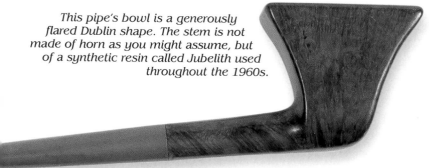

A briar pipe's quality is determined by experts. The top-of-the-line are straight grain and bird's eye, both rarities. A notch lower is first choice, or "extra." This "extra" model has a bold bulldog shape.

The tradition of handmade pipe making still exists today. It is often passed down from generation to generation. This pipe was made by hand at the Saint-Claude house of EWA. EWA was founded in 1809 by Horace Waille, who passed the business on to his son René in 1902, who gave it over to his son René Waille in 1932. In 1974 it went to the next in line, Michel, who is still in charge today.

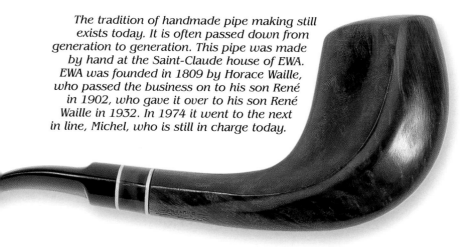

No two handmade
pipes are alike. Well
before execution, each
piece demands a range
of artistic decisions,
including the specific
briarwood to be used,
and the fabrication methods.
Each one really is an
independent work of sculpture.
This freehand pipe, signed Chacom,
was made in the 1970s.

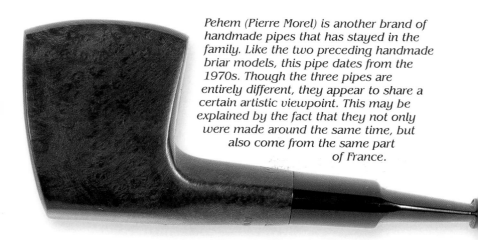

Pehem (Pierre Morel) is another brand of handmade pipes that has stayed in the family. Like the two preceding handmade briar models, this pipe dates from the 1970s. Though the three pipes are entirely different, they appear to share a certain artistic viewpoint. This may be explained by the fact that they not only were made around the same time, but also come from the same part of France.

This is another Pehem pipe from the 1970s. The wood grain was clearly decisive in the artist's choice of form. The grain is further emphasized by the rugged surface handling.

A fine specimen of rare bird's eye briar. Bird's eye is so hard to come by that the denomination is no longer officially used. This model was also made by hand in the 1970s.

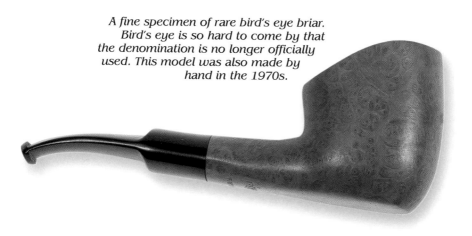

This elegantly sloped freehand briar
also dates from the 1970s.
Traditionally freehands refer to pipes in
which no machine is used, except,
possibly a turning lathe for holding the
wood. In the 1950s the Danish led the
way in renewing the term's original
meaning: hand carving with no
formal preconceptions but to follow
the grain. The 1970s were
a freehand
heyday.

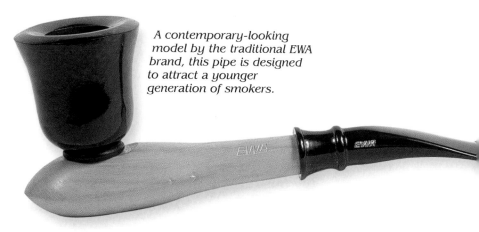

A contemporary-looking model by the traditional EWA brand, this pipe is designed to attract a younger generation of smokers.

The Volute pipe by Claude Robin, one of the pipe designers asked to create commemorative models in 1996, on the occasion of the thirtieth anniversary of the Saint-Claude brotherhood of master pipe makers.

*This streamlined, racy model in silver-plated
briarwood was made for a very old pipe
manufacturer, Jeantet, founded in 1775.
Jeantet at first specialized in selling all
sorts of wood objects before branching
out into clay pipe stems and then
finally specializing in pipes.*

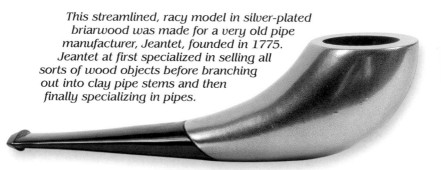

Pourquoi Pas? (Why Not?) is the name given to this Chap brand pipe, designed by Erwin van Handenhoven. It is made of briarwood set in a molded synthetic resin, to pack an electrically elegant blue punch.

The top French pipe manufacturers got together and came up with the novel idea of a line of pastel blue models. The ten snazzy pipes in the Pastel 2000 collection have great names too: Steam (below), Ulysse (facing page, left) Fun Bleu (facing page, right), Tulip, Cyclade, and so on. The participating brands were Butz-Choquin, Chacom, Chap, Jeantet, EWA, and Ropp.

These two Italian pipes come from Castello, a top manufacturer that is a special favorite among U.S. collectors. Castello was started in 1947 by Carlo Scotti. It produces only freehand pipes, using unique methods. This straight-grained briar beauty has a raised, sandblasted stem.

Castello was taken over by Carlo Scotti's assistant Franco Coppo, who maintained the original house rule of never expanding the workshop beyond five artisans. This stunning model, like the majority of Castello pipes, is fashioned from the finest Ligurian briar. The ivory inlay in the plexiglass stem is Castello's signature.

The Irish pipe master Charles Peterson went to work for the Kapp brand in 1890. Peterson came up with many innovations, including a reservoir carved into the top of the pipe's head to seal in the "pipe juce" given off in combustion. Peterson also invented a stem designed to direct the smoke to the palate, not the tongue. This century-old manufacturer created a handsome Sherlock Holmes line in 1990.

*This Dunhill
model is the height of
understated elegance. Dunhill pipes are
made from only the finest quality briar. This makes
them cost a pretty penny, but many a smoker
considers it money well spent.*

*This Dunhill pipe is
less traditional at first
glance, with this sterling silver
ring mount and stained, sandblasted
briarwood. But a classic is always a classic.*

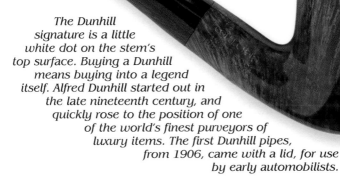

The Dunhill
signature is a little
white dot on the stem's
top surface. Buying a Dunhill
means buying into a legend
itself. Alfred Dunhill started out in
the late nineteenth century, and
quickly rose to the position of one
of the world's finest purveyors of
luxury items. The first Dunhill pipes,
from 1906, came with a lid, for use
by early automobilists.

Up until about five hundred years ago, an immense oak forest flourished north of the Loire River in France. The forest was flooded by the ocean, leaving fossilized oak under layers of peat. The fossilized wood is deep ebony colored, with the added beauty of veins. Patrice Sébilo, the only remaining master pipe maker in western France, has dedicated his craft to this rare material.

The fossilized wood is called morta. Pipe aficionados claim that it combines the solidity of briarwood with a taste worthy of meerschaum.

II

FIGURATIVE
pipes

There is such a variety of pipes with human faces, it seems that one exists for every historical or mythical type. And these pipes are perhaps the most fun to stumble upon. Clay is the commonest material for such portraits in miniature and, through the centuries, new models have constantly appeared. The competition is stiff, so creativity and a sense of novelty are high. Manufacturers have been known to copy one another's work, making for variants that catch a collector's eye. With famous and forgotten figures, from fact to fantasy, this chapter presents a pipe-dream version of history.

Briarwood and horn are used here to model the head of Christ. This late-nineteenth-century pipe does not sacrifice its classic shape to its figurative subject.

The French pipe maker Gambier had stopped production in the 1920s, but still had thousands of pipes stored in the basement. At the end of World War II, as the American army moved through France, this stock was dumped into the street and crushed beneath approaching tanks. Many Christs like this one probably suffered the consequences.

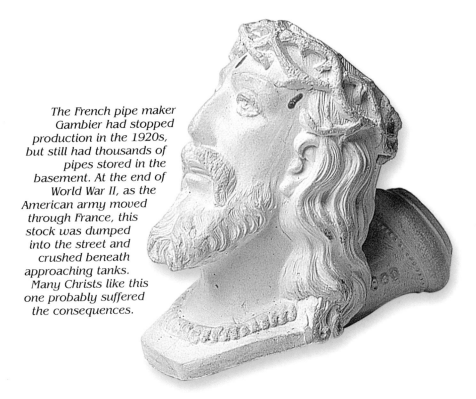

This little silver pipe depicts a Roman soldier's head.
It dates back to the seventeenth century, and was
made in either England or France. The tiny ring was
for a chain that attached to the missing stem.

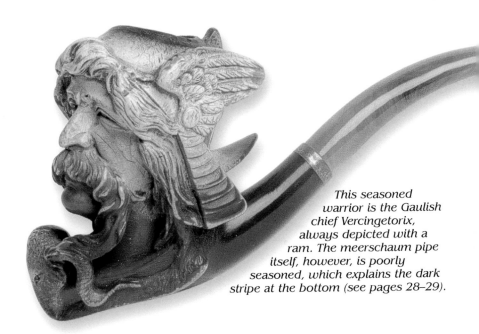

This seasoned warrior is the Gaulish chief Vercingetorix, always depicted with a ram. The meerschaum pipe itself, however, is poorly seasoned, which explains the dark stripe at the bottom (see pages 28–29).

This pipe is meant to represent the legendary Bayard, the most perfect of all French knights. The Gambier rendition doesn't quite seem to capture Bayard's chivalrous refinement, but imbues him with more stolid aggressiveness.

Joan of Arc—another French warrior, and much better known although she was just a young girl. Yet since she was burnt at the stake, smoking her image may be of somewhat poor taste.

This is the great Portuguese explorer Vasco de Gama, who sailed around the Cape of Good Hope in 1498, as the schoolbooks say.

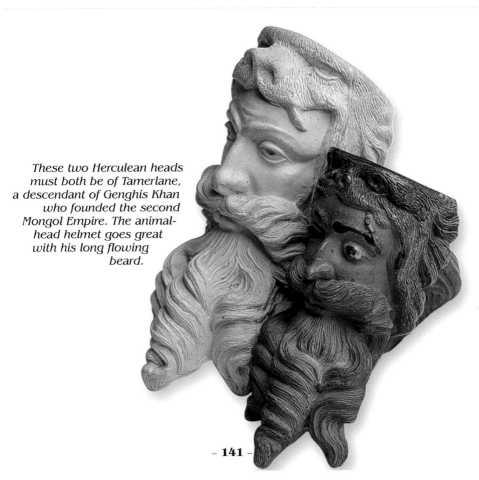

These two Herculean heads must both be of Tamerlane, a descendant of Genghis Khan who founded the second Mongol Empire. The animal-head helmet goes great with his long flowing beard.

This Gambier bowl is a portrait of Henri IV, the French king who was assassinated in 1610. The facing page shows the famously beheaded Marie Antoinette.

It was first made by Cretal-Gallard around 1820, and turned out to be one of the most popular clay pipe models through the early twentieth century. Another case of bad taste?

These historical pipes both represent men who led insurrections against the French Revolution. Here we have François de Charette. He was known in the 1790s as "the King of the Vendée" when he led peasants into battle. The pipes date to about a century later.

The peasants of the Vendée insurrection objected to the Revolution's turning against the Catholic Church, and they supported their local nobility. This pipe head represents their commander, Henri La Rochejaquelein, famous for saying, "If I advance, follow me. If I retreat, do me in. If I'm killed, take revenge."

French Revolutionary figures have inspired many pipe heads. This is clearly a tricoteuse or knitter, one of the simple women who attended Revolutionary meetings, knitting needles in hand. Royalists called them the "furies of the guillotine."

This is Charlotte Corday, another French Revolutionary figure, much lovlier than her sister on the facing page. She is remembered for assassinating Marat in his bathtub.

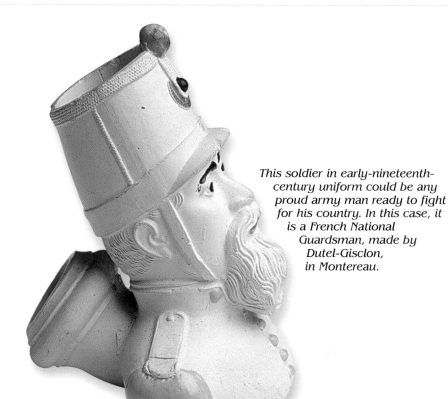

This soldier in early-nineteenth-century uniform could be any proud army man ready to fight for his country. In this case, it is a French National Guardsman, made by Dutel-Gisclon, in Montereau.

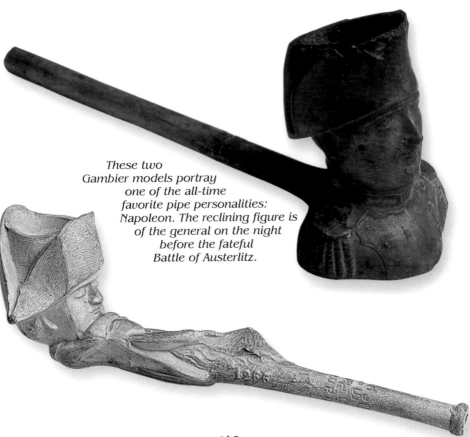

These two
Gambier models portray
one of the all-time
favorite pipe personalities:
Napoleon. The reclining figure is
of the general on the night
before the fateful
Battle of Austerlitz.

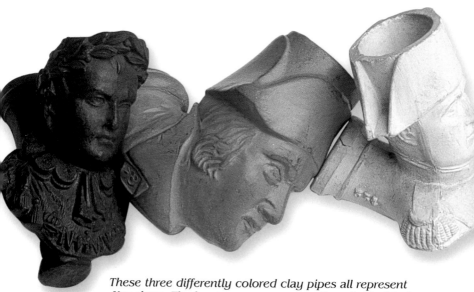

These three differently colored clay pipes all represent
Napoleon. The least common among them is the black
pipe whose color was acquired either by a second firing
in sawdust, or by being stained by smoke. The red pipe
in the middle comes from Turkey, but a nearly identical
model was also popular in Italy.

After all, Napoleon did set out to conquer the world. Here he is again, on the eve of his invasion of Italy. Pipe makers have their trade secrets. But it is known that this wood patina was usually achieved by soaking the bowl in non-pasteurized whole milk before a second firing.

This briar Napoleon is much more recent, dating from around 1985. It is the work of the master pipe sculptor Paul Lanier.

This finely composed bowl portrays Prince Józef Anton Poniatowski, nicknamed the Polish Bayard for his perfect soldiery and loyalty to his commander. The commander in question was of course Napoleon. Poniatowski distinguished himself during Napoleon's grueling Russian campaign.

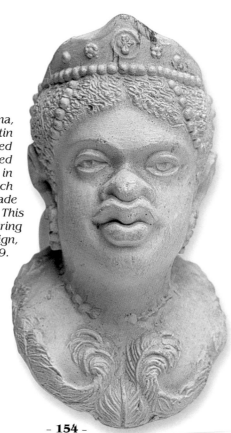

This is Her Highness Adelina, the wife of Faustin Soulouque, a self-styled Napoleon who proclaimed himself Emperor of Haiti in 1847. His courtiers bore such titles as the Duke of Lemonade and Count Number Two. This pipe was made during Soulouque's short reign, which ended in 1859.

*Like all things
Chinese, African
subjects appealed to the European thirst for
exoticism in the eighteenth and nineteenth centuries.
These twin heads were made by two different French
firms, Bonnaud and Job-Clerc. The manufacturers
clearly shared their molds.*

Clay pipes were first made in England, at the beginning of the seventeenth century. The technique spread to Holland when a refugee fleeing political and religious strife in England settled in Gouda. The black of this English pipe is only skin deep; white can be detected underneath in the chipped spots.

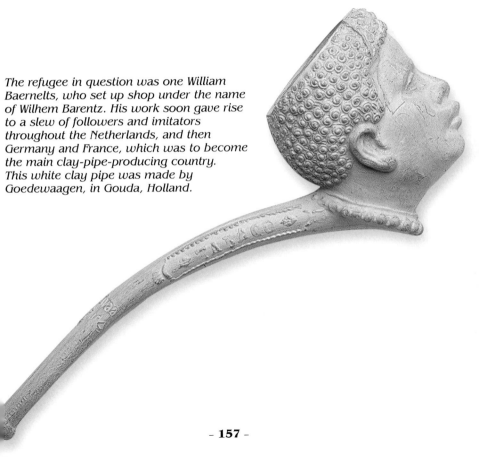

The refugee in question was one William Baernelts, who set up shop under the name of Wilhem Barentz. His work soon gave rise to a slew of followers and imitators throughout the Netherlands, and then Germany and France, which was to become the main clay-pipe-producing country. This white clay pipe was made by Goedewaagen, in Gouda, Holland.

Here are two more pipe heads with African features. The black one is by an unknown maker, while the white is signed Dutel-Gisclon. The string wound around the bit of the black pipe served to protect the smoker's teeth.

This amusing head, with its missing lid, was designed for the smoke to go out of the face's mouth. It is probably from the late nineteenth century, by an unknown manufacturer.

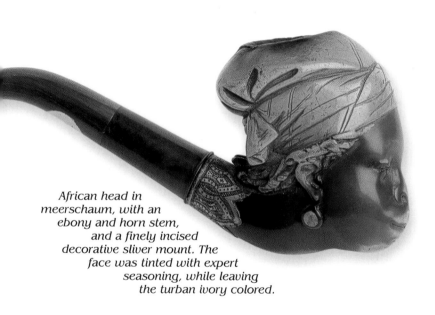

African head in
meerschaum, with an
ebony and horn stem,
and a finely incised
decorative sliver mount. The
face was tinted with expert
seasoning, while leaving
the turban ivory colored.

This is a nineteenth-century meerschaum likeness of Abd ar-Rahman, a Muslim governor of Spain and also a warrior who was defeated in France in 732 by Charles Martel. Arabic themes, like African ones, also captured the European imagination of the time.

A rare red clay pipe depicting Kemal Atatürk, who founded modern Turkey in 1923. The maker may be Fiolet. The loop at the bottom was for attaching the bowl to the stem.

This vividly sculpted late-nineteenth-century Saint-Claude head is of a horseman from the Hejaz district of the Saudi peninsula. The stem is in horn.

The names of a good many nineteenth-century pipe makers and shops took inspiration from Middle-Eastern themes. A few of these establishments are still in business today. This pipe's vertical shape is reminiscent of a hookah.

This Saxony porcelain marvel from Germany has a silver lid and ferule mount. The horn stem is adorned with a thin pompom cord. Turbaned heads with not particularly Arab features were commonly portrayed on German pipes.

Asian figures provided yet
another "exotic" pipe topic.
This imposing Gambier
Mandarin measures 4¾ inches
(12 cm) and is a hot
collector's item. Warrior
though he is, he stands
holding a fan, not a weapon,
and his expression is not so
ferocious, though you
couldn't exactly call
it friendly.

*These two Gambier pipes feature a Chinese porter
and a prisoner. The stem of the prisoner pipe has
two conduits; one goes through each of his legs.*

The military cap of the meerschaum officer on the bowl dates this model to 1870, while the infantryman on the stem wears an 1850s uniform. As with all fine meerschaum pipes, the case is also a work of art. Cases were carved from a single piece of wood, often linden, split into two equal parts, and carved out to fit the pipe like a sculpture in the negative. They were then covered with leather on the outside and lined with satin or velvet. Today cases are machine-made from wood compounds.

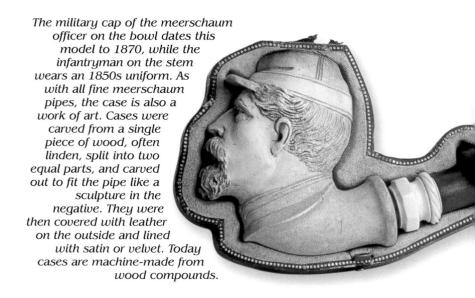

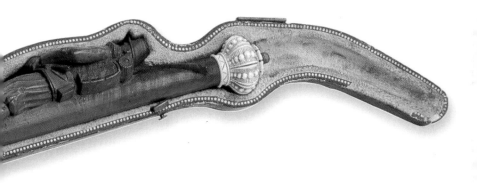

Having your face on a pipe could be a sign of public popularity. Pipes with the head of General Georges Boulanger, the leader of an authoritarian populist movement in France, disappeared from store display cases after he fled to Belgium in 1889 and committed suicide on his mistress's grave.

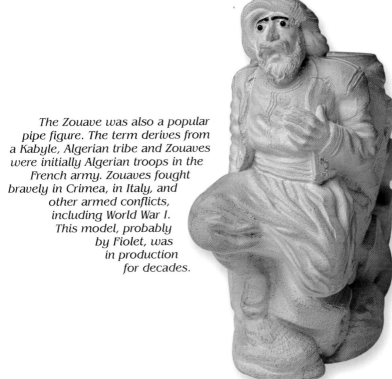

The Zouave was also a popular pipe figure. The term derives from a Kabyle, Algerian tribe and Zouaves were initially Algerian troops in the French army. Zouaves fought bravely in Crimea, in Italy, and other armed conflicts, including World War I. This model, probably by Fiolet, was in production for decades.

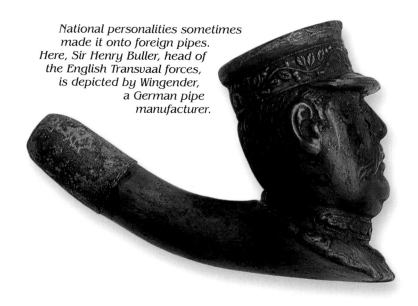

National personalities sometimes made it onto foreign pipes. Here, Sir Henry Buller, head of the English Transvaal forces, is depicted by Wingender, a German pipe manufacturer.

Another internationally-inspired head, Franz Josef of Austria is portrayed by the French pipe maker Job-Clerc. The green patina of the bronze cap lends an almost sporting air here.

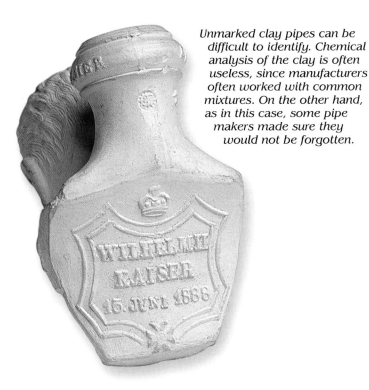

Unmarked clay pipes can be difficult to identify. Chemical analysis of the clay is often useless, since manufacturers often worked with common mixtures. On the other hand, as in this case, some pipe makers made sure they would not be forgotten.

This is the German Kaiser Wilhelm II, portrayed by Gambier in France. The date of the ruler's accession to the throne, June 15, 1888, is marked in German, indicating that the French manufacturer had an eye to exportation. The only thing missing is the date of his defeat and exile, 1918.

Political cartoon of a pipe showing the vanquished Czar Nicolas of Russia literally spitting out his Crimean War losses: Sebastopol, Alma, Balaklava. The head is firmly held down by two hands, one marked England and the other, France.

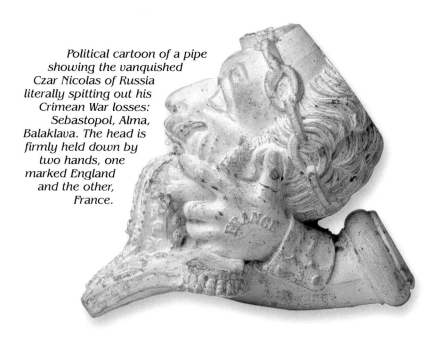

King Leopold II of Belgium was a pacifist who devoted his energies to gaining neutrality for his country in 1870. Greatly respected by posterity, he was not so popular among his own people. This pipe was designed for international consumption.

The end of the clay pipe's heyday coincided with World War I, just in time to capture the likenesses of bearded soldiers like this one, sculpted by Jacques Loysel. The clay pipe was replaced by briar models, or forgotten altogether for cigarettes.

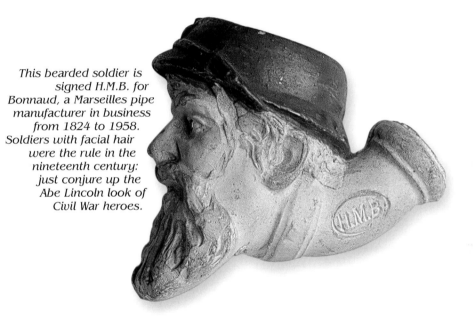

This bearded soldier is signed H.M.B. for Bonnaud, a Marseilles pipe manufacturer in business from 1824 to 1958. Soldiers with facial hair were the rule in the nineteenth century: just conjure up the Abe Lincoln look of Civil War heroes.

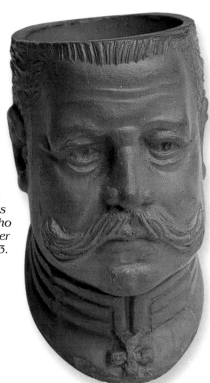

Paul von Beneckendorff und von Hindenburg was a German commander defeated by the French in 1918. He went on, however, to be elected president of the Weimar Republic in 1925, and was reelected in 1932. It was Hindenburg who nominated Hitler chancellor in 1933.

The head of Marshal Joseph Joffre is topped with what appears to be an old-fashioned and impractical pirate hat. The subject was nevertheless a successful French commander through World War I. This pipe was made by Job-Clerc, the very last French manufacturer of clay pipes, which closed in 1970.

With the end of World War I, and the thrill of victory for the Allies, heroes' faces dominated pipe bowls.

Popular among them were King Albert I of Belgium (left), his wife the queen, Joffre, and Marshal Ferdinand Foch (facing page).

The models on this double page are both Belgian. They are made of glazed clay, and were probably designed as souvenirs rather than for smoking. Pipe smokers prefer porous clay.

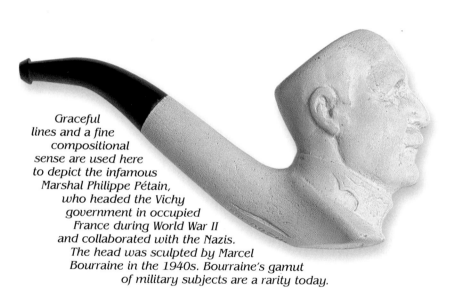

Graceful
lines and a fine
compositional
sense are used here
to depict the infamous
Marshal Philippe Pétain,
who headed the Vichy
government in occupied
France during World War II
and collaborated with the Nazis.
The head was sculpted by Marcel
Bourraine in the 1940s. Bourraine's gamut
of military subjects are a rarity today.

Here is a majestic Marianne, symbol of the French spirit. Her Phrygian cap and rooster are partially colored. Such added color is rare for meerschaum pipes.

Jacob is an all time favorite among pipe heads, to the point where for a while all clay pipes were affectionately called "Jacob." There were so many imitations of the original Gambier model from the 1830s, that the manufacturer added "I am a real Jacob" on the turban.

But this in no way put off Gambier's imitators, who also blazoned the turbans of their Jacobs. This one is called "Old Jacob." It was made by Levesque in Andenne, Belgium.

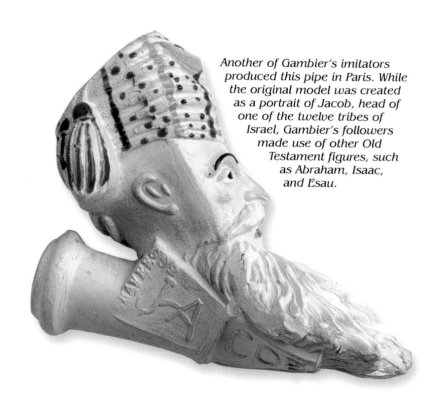

Another of Gambier's imitators produced this pipe in Paris. While the original model was created as a portrait of Jacob, head of one of the twelve tribes of Israel, Gambier's followers made use of other Old Testament figures, such as Abraham, Isaac, and Esau.

This pipe's headdress is blazoned "The Real Abraham"! It is a copy made by the Trees company of Belgium. You can also find the "It's Me, the Fine Jacob" model, made by Fiolet and Schmidt Frères, "It's Me, the Worthy Jacob" by Dutel-Gisclon, "The New Jacob" by Job-Clerc, and even "I am the True Jacob" by Wingender!

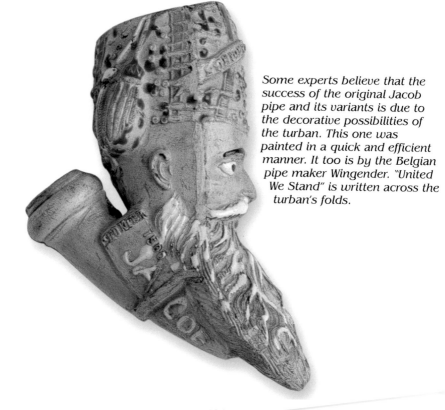

Some experts believe that the success of the original Jacob pipe and its variants is due to the decorative possibilities of the turban. This one was painted in a quick and efficient manner. It too is by the Belgian pipe maker Wingender. "United We Stand" is written across the turban's folds.

But even copies that are not glazed have their advantages. In this red clay model by Bonnaud Jacob's beard is designed so that you can hold the pipe without burning your fingers.

None of these pipes claim to be Jacobs per se. But the success of Jacob pipes certainly inspired their creation. From left to right: The Turk and Jupiter by Gambier, another Jupiter by Dutel-Gisclon, and then a Gambier Saturn.

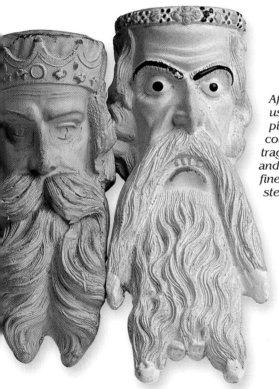

After firing in kilns, women usually decorated this sort of pipe. They mixed their own colors with a combination of tragacanth, varnishing powder and water, and applied them with fine brushes and very narrow steel pointers before re-firing.

At left, two of Gambier's magnificent clay Bacchuses. The head at right is carved in briar. Both meerschaum and wood sculptors of mythological topics often took inspiration from clay models. In the nineteenth century, competition among pipe makers was fierce. This led pipe sculptors to work intensely at polishing their artistry in the execution of favorite topics.

These pipes were known as "Village Husbands." The one at left was made by Blanc-Garin, the other by Gambier. Blanc-Garin was founded in 1834 and purchased by Gambier in 1860.

It has been claimed, but never proven, that the painter and sculptor Honoré Daumier and the sculptor of the Statue of Liberty, Frédéric Auguste Bartholdi worked for Gambier. However, it is certain that the sculptor Jean-Pierre Dantan was in their employ—this bowl is a self-portrait/caricature of the artist! The famous French Romantic writer Théophile Gautier said that Dantan was "the sculptor who is best at manifesting facial expressions in plaster. Sculpture is the most serious of arts, and he makes it laugh."

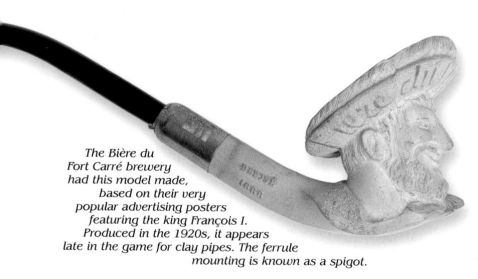

The Bière du
Fort Carré brewery
had this model made,
based on their very
popular advertising posters
featuring the king François I.
Produced in the 1920s, it appears
late in the game for clay pipes. The ferrule
mounting is known as a spigot.

It may come as a surprise that so many pipes appear on these pages without stems. But, as a matter of fact, the primary interest of the pipe collector is the bowl. Before the advent of ebonite, lips were made of horn or bone, and bowls were mainly made of cherry wood and bamboo. In pipes that do not use a spigot system, the head and stem are held together with cork and wedged into rims like the one beneath this head.

A woman from Normandy and a German military student. Both of these pipes come from Gambier. The region in France near the Belgian border where Gambier produced its pipes is famous for its white clay.

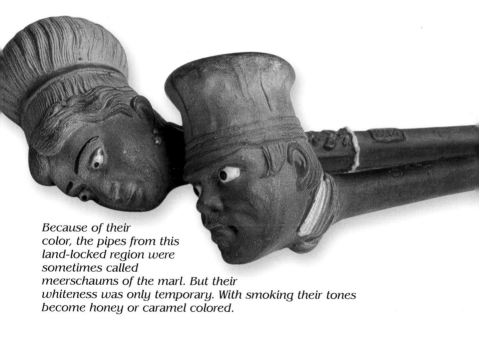

Because of their
color, the pipes from this
land-locked region were
sometimes called
meerschaums of the marl. But their
whiteness was only temporary. With smoking their tones
become honey or caramel colored.

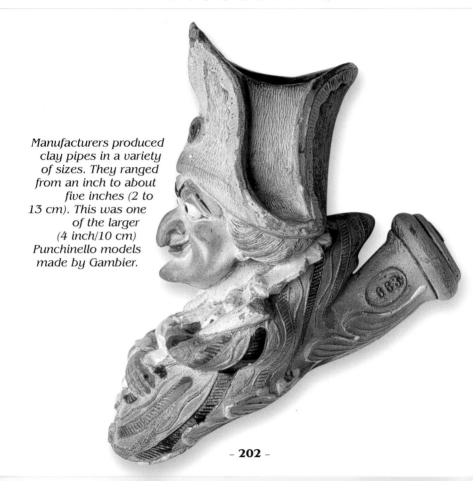

Manufacturers produced clay pipes in a variety of sizes. They ranged from an inch to about five inches (2 to 13 cm). This was one of the larger (4 inch/10 cm) Punchinello models made by Gambier.

Note how smoking has brought out the white glaze on this 2¾ inch (7 cm) Gambier bowl. New, it would have been nearly invisible. Some collectors prefer seasoned to mint-condition pipes.

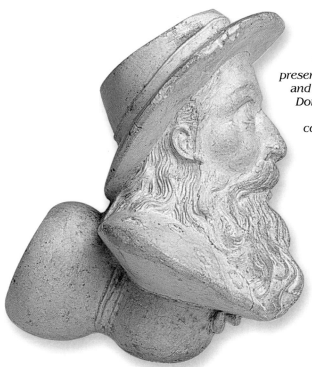

These two pages present Cervantes (left) and his famous hero, Don Quixote, knight of the woeful countenance. Both bowls are the work of Dutel-Gisclon.

Dutel-Gisclon was founded in Northern France's white clay region, and then moved just southeast of Paris in 1870, where much porcelain work was being done at the time. Some pipe aficionados have complained ever since that the results do not have the same sparkle and whiteness.

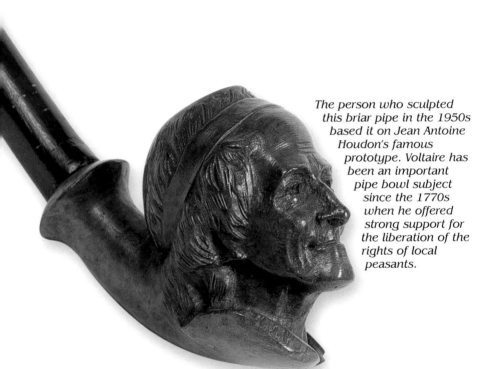

The person who sculpted this briar pipe in the 1950s based it on Jean Antoine Houdon's famous prototype. Voltaire has been an important pipe bowl subject since the 1770s when he offered strong support for the liberation of the rights of local peasants.

Gambier pipe makers were true art lovers. Witness these two models, representing Rembrandt and Rubens. In fact, their catalogue featured more than two thousand different heads.

This pipe bowl was sculpted by Paul Lanier with the head of the composer Hector Berlioz. The model dates from the 1990s.

Another Paul Lanier creation, this time of Chopin. Lanier is usually commissioned to create his pipes. These two can be seen at the Musée de la Pipe et du Diamant (see page 374).

This fine pipe dates to the end of the nineteenth century. It is made of a single piece of briarwood, with an amber mouthpiece. Note the skilled rendering of the sarcasm on the face of Mephistopheles, the demon who tempted Faust with universal knowledge.

The Job-Leclerc factory may have used this model for more than one purpose. Is it Victor Hugo or Giuseppe Verdi?

The pipe smoker's antipathy to cigarettes had to be overcome in this case. The poetic French pop singer and composer Serge Gainsbourg was an inveterate cigarette smoker.

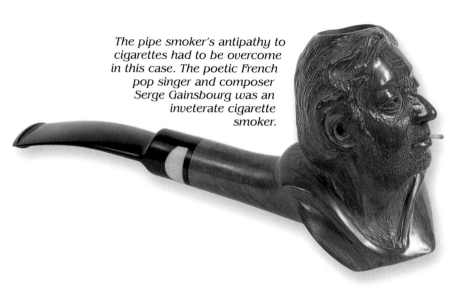

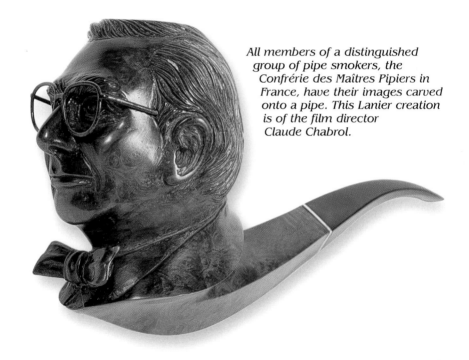

All members of a distinguished group of pipe smokers, the Confrérie des Maîtres Pipiers in France, have their images carved onto a pipe. This Lanier creation is of the film director Claude Chabrol.

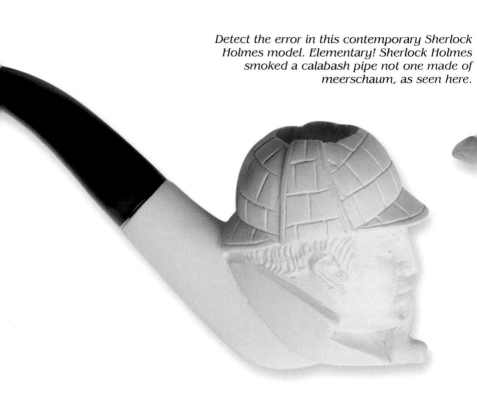

Detect the error in this contemporary Sherlock Holmes model. Elementary! Sherlock Holmes smoked a calabash pipe not one made of meerschaum, as seen here.

Both the detective model and that of Doctor Watson (below) were made in Turkey. International laws limiting the exportation of raw meerschaum have been on the books since 1961.

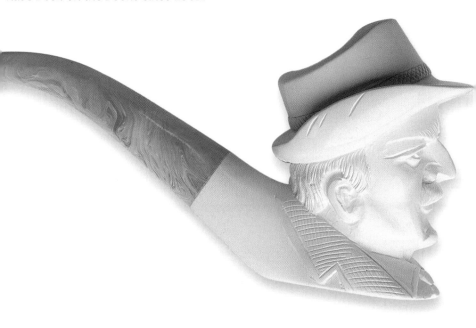

Locomotive engineer? World War I flying ace? Or is it Douglas Fairbanks?

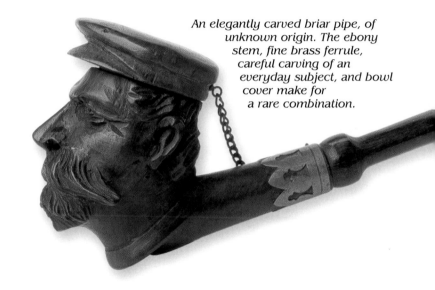

An elegantly carved briar pipe, of unknown origin. The ebony stem, fine brass ferrule, careful carving of an everyday subject, and bowl cover make for a rare combination.

The Old Man, wise
or otherwise, is a
frequent pipe subject.
This is a late-nineteenth-
century briar pipe; the bit
and lip are in ebonite.

A superb example from Vienna, Austria, this meerschaum was manufactured in the second half of the nineteenth century. Like Jacob pipe models (see pages 186–91), the beard serves as a perfect grip.

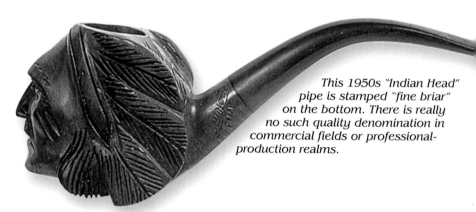

This 1950s "Indian Head" pipe is stamped "fine briar" on the bottom. There is really no such quality denomination in commercial fields or professional-production realms.

Curiously, this German porcelain bowl and shank represents a man smoking a Dutch-style pipe. It is comprised of an interesting array of materials as well.

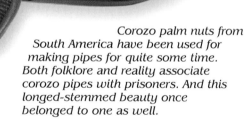

Corozo palm nuts from South America have been used for making pipes for quite some time. Both folklore and reality associate corozo pipes with prisoners. And this longed-stemmed beauty once belonged to one as well.

As the Belgian surrealist painter René Magritte put it in another context, "This is not a pipe." It is a rare snuff box with a caricature from the nineteenth century, courtesy of the Saint-Claude Pipe Museum.

This too is not a pipe, but a form used in pipe manufacture. It is made of a zinc and aluminum alloy, and was used in a process perfected by Henry Dalloz in 1863. The output was then hand painted and ready for sale.

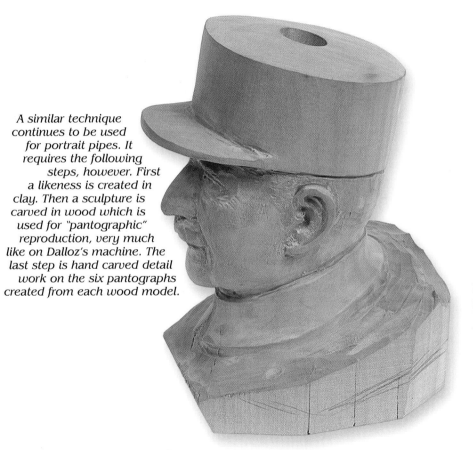

A similar technique continues to be used for portrait pipes. It requires the following steps, however. First a likeness is created in clay. Then a sculpture is carved in wood which is used for "pantographic" reproduction, very much like on Dalloz's machine. The last step is hand carved detail work on the six pantographs created from each wood model.

III

ANIMAL
pipes

P ipe artists have always taken inspiration from the animal kingdom. In addition to domestic favorites such as frisky lapdogs and elegant racehorses, idyllic cows and crowing cocks, they have also sculpted and painted a great variety of exotic animals—some of which existed only in some sculptor's imagination. Whether tender, ferocious, or funny, our selection includes a menagerie of these surprising creations by eighteenth-century artists who may never have seen their subjects in the flesh.

This perky cat was created by the Fiolet company. An 1846 Fiolet catalog describes its factory as the largest in Europe. At that time Fiolet had 800 employees and manufactured more than 160,000 pipes a day.

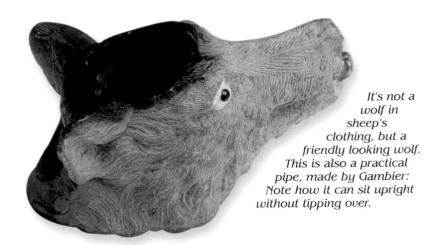

It's not a wolf in sheep's clothing, but a friendly looking wolf. This is also a practical pipe, made by Gambier: Note how it can sit upright without tipping over.

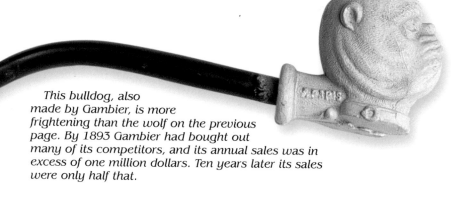

This bulldog, also
made by Gambier, is more
frightening than the wolf on the previous
page. By 1893 Gambier had bought out
many of its competitors, and its annual sales was in
excess of one million dollars. Ten years later its sales
were only half that.

The small model poodle by
Gambier and the bulldog by Fiolet
are accompanied by a Hungarian
cigarette holder featuring,
you guessed it, a Hungarian
Vizsla hound.

*This too is a cigarette holder.
It is very finely crafted,
as is its made-to-order
padded case.*

Here we have the hound's head
as well as the hunter's horn.
This pipe was made by
Duméril-Leurs.

*This small model pipe bowl in the shape of a
wild boar's head was made by Noël artisans
whose workshop was founded in 1834 in
Lyon, France. Noël too was bought out by
Gambier in 1890. If you come across Noël
pipes stamped with "Paris" or other city
names, don't be misled. Such indications were
merely cast for added cachet.*

Notice the small hunter standing in the antlers on this hunter's pipe. The model dates to the beginning of the nineteenth century. Its lid has been lost.

Boxwood and elm root were very common pipe-making materials before the widespread use of porcelain, especially in Germany. German pipes carved from these materials are known as Ulms, named after the city in southwestern Germany. Note the deer ambling about in the pine forest. The pipe is clearly dated, August 1754, and has a silver top.

This gentleman fox probably hails from early-nineteenth-century Bohemia. You can come across dogs, eagles, roosters, parrots, and other animals in the same style. See the bear on page 268.

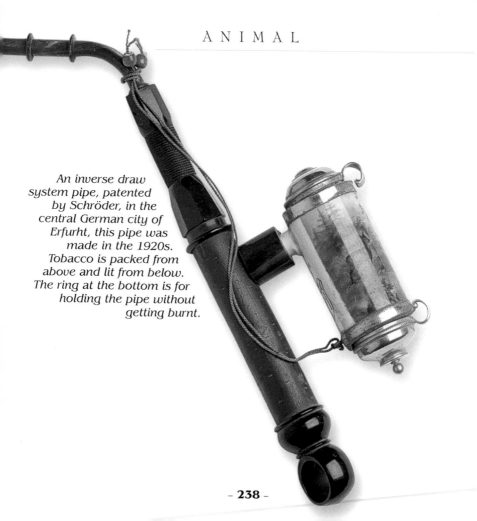

An inverse draw system pipe, patented by Schröder, in the central German city of Erfurht, this pipe was made in the 1920s. Tobacco is packed from above and lit from below. The ring at the bottom is for holding the pipe without getting burnt.

Raymond Monneret was a virtuoso at sculpting deer scenes. He signed his works "Monn" and he loved working in briar. This piece was carved in the 1950s.

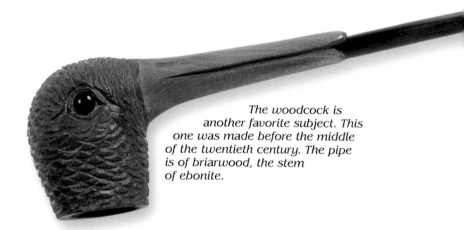

The woodcock is
another favorite subject. This
one was made before the middle
of the twentieth century. The pipe
is of briarwood, the stem
of ebonite.

Here we have a meerschaum woodcock. It was restored by Philippe Bargiel, an internationally recognized specialist in the domain.

The white rooster pipe is a Gambier, the brown a Noël, two pipe-makers who eventually merged (see page 234). Note the different glazing techniques.

The brown pipe is a Gambier, the more ivory-toned model is by Scouflaire. This type of model is known as a Cock's Claw.

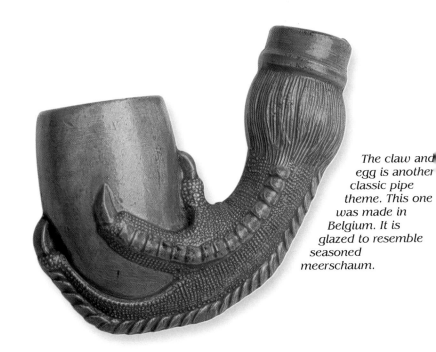

The claw and egg is another classic pipe theme. This one was made in Belgium. It is glazed to resemble seasoned meerschaum.

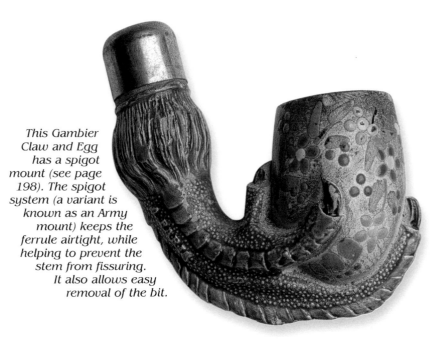

This Gambier Claw and Egg has a spigot mount (see page 198). The spigot system (a variant is known as an Army mount) keeps the ferrule airtight, while helping to prevent the stem from fissuring. It also allows easy removal of the bit.

This is a real meerschaum Cock and Egg, probably from nineteenth-century Austria. The horn stem, on the other hand, was made in France.

Anyone who collects claw models will
certainly have his or her hands full! This
briarwood pipe dates from the turn of the
twentieth century. The stem is made of
ebonite, a product derived from
the Amazonian hevea tree
(see page 100).

When Gambier made simpler models, such as this bird-shaped pipe, the company used bronze mold forms comprised of two pieces. For a human face or other more complex subjects, three part forms were required.

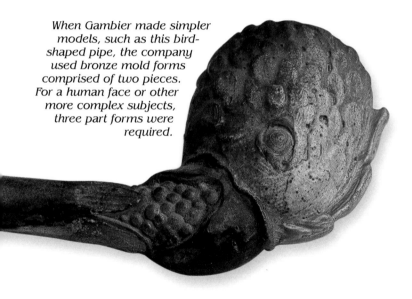

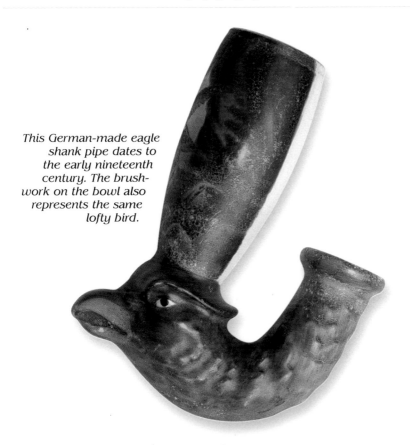

This German-made eagle shank pipe dates to the early nineteenth century. The brushwork on the bowl also represents the same lofty bird.

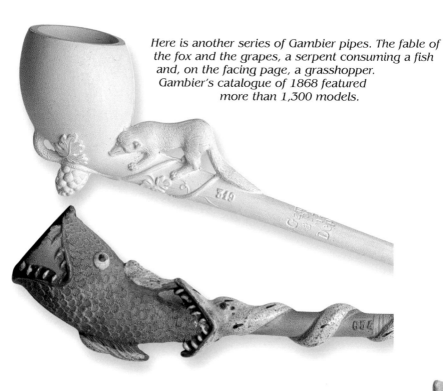

Here is another series of Gambier pipes. The fable of
the fox and the grapes, a serpent consuming a fish
and, on the facing page, a grasshopper.
Gambier's catalogue of 1868 featured
more than 1,300 models.

This fine enamel work pipe dates to the first half of the nineteenth century. Once again the heel has been shaped like a fly (see page 90).

Fiolet made this "Gambon" pipe. The name derives from a nineteenth-century news story about a man named Gambon who insisted upon paying his taxes in livestock.

This large bull was sculpted in Saint-Claude, France, near the turn of the twentieth century. The head is more than 5 inches (13 cm) tall, and it measures 6 inches (15 cm) from nose to shank. And yes, you guessed it, his horns are made of horn.

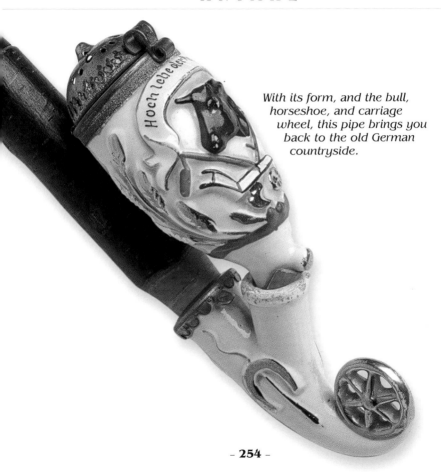

With its form, and the bull, horseshoe, and carriage wheel, this pipe brings you back to the old German countryside.

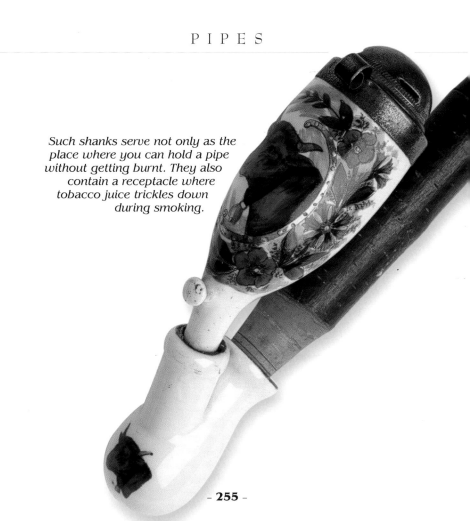

Such shanks serve not only as the place where you can hold a pipe without getting burnt. They also contain a receptacle where tobacco juice trickles down during smoking.

The pipe at left is dated 1889, and the one at right is probably its very close contemporary. Both are German. The shanks are lost, and may have displayed other historically or artistically interesting factors.

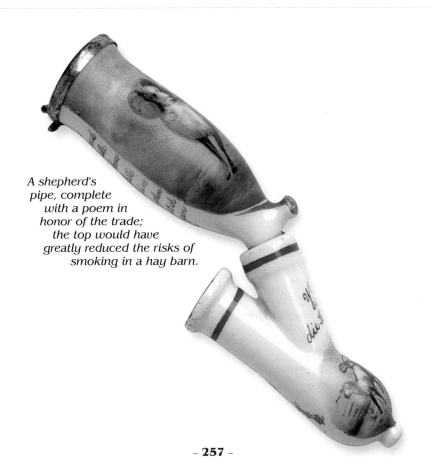

A shepherd's pipe, complete with a poem in honor of the trade; the top would have greatly reduced the risks of smoking in a hay barn.

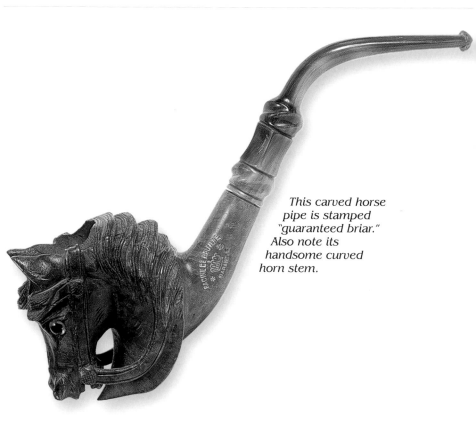

This carved horse pipe is stamped "guaranteed briar." Also note its handsome curved horn stem.

Famous Austrian Lipizzan horses? In any case,
this late-nineteenth-century Austrian pipe
presents two horses in a graceful duet—
accompanied by an elegant amber bit and lip.

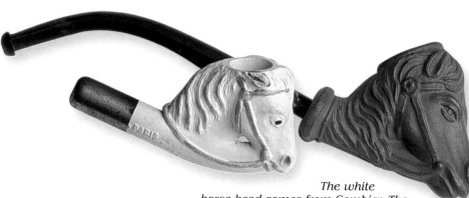

*The white
horse head comes from Gambier. The
red clay horse is the work of Job-Clerc. The
latter has an ebonite stem, but during the
nineteenth century bowls like these were usually
mounted on bamboo stems of various lengths
(see page 289), with horn or bone lips,
depending on the smoker's taste and/or means.*

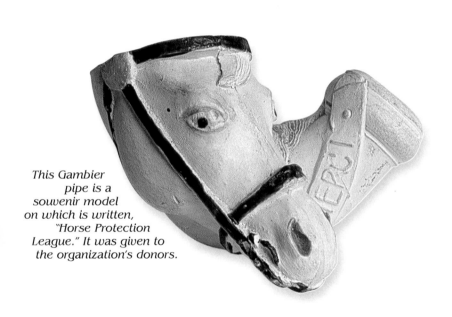

This Gambier pipe is a souvenir model on which is written, "Horse Protection League." It was given to the organization's donors.

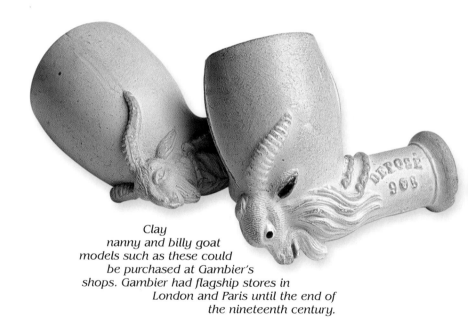

Clay
nanny and billy goat
models such as these could
be purchased at Gambier's
shops. Gambier had flagship stores in
London and Paris until the end of
the nineteenth century.

*Although
he looks a little
awkward, this briar pig
has the advantage of
being able to stand on his
own four feet. Many pipes tip
when you put them down.*

It is very difficult to find a pipe like this one in such fine condition. It's another Gambier, this time in the Art Nouveau style at the start of the twentieth century.

The shape of the snail shell is a tempting challenge for the pipe artist. The model also dates to the beginning of the twentieth century (see pages 328–329).

Like the pipes on pages 276–281, this one is the work of Paul Lanier. This little monkey measures about 3⅛ inches (8 cm).

This is not your run-of-the-mill chimp. It's Gambier's representation of the monkey that belonged to the Empress Eugenie, Napoleon III's consort.

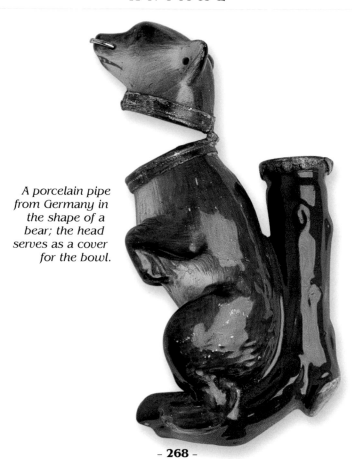

A porcelain pipe from Germany in the shape of a bear; the head serves as a cover for the bowl.

Up through the Renaissance it was believed that bear cubs were born as a kind of unformed mass to be licked into shape by the mother bear. The origins of this pipe are unknown, and the kind of wood in which it is carved has not yet been identified.

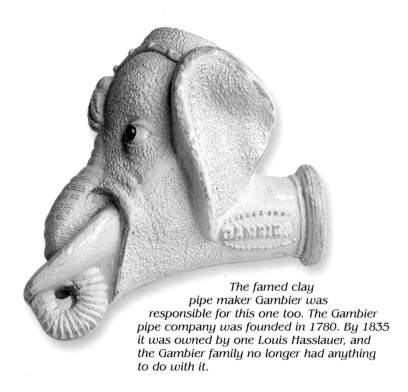

The famed clay pipe maker Gambier was responsible for this one too. The Gambier pipe company was founded in 1780. By 1835 it was owned by one Louis Hasslauer, and the Gambier family no longer had anything to do with it.

This pipe hails from Switzerland. It represents a more elongated version of the lion on a Lucerne monument commemorating a 1792 conflict.

It shouldn't be surprising to find many pipes sporting the king of the animal world. This one dates to the early 1900s.

This ferocious beast by Gambier dates to the days when rising public figures and celebrities were frequently referred to as lions. The origin of this practice is apparently the Tower of London's lions, which attracted much attention at the time.

It looks like a lion, but then again it has deer-like limbs. Whether it is meant to be a whimsical or mythological creature, or is simply a misconceived lion, the overall effect is quite charming.

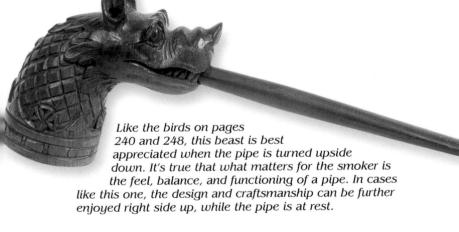

Like the birds on pages 240 and 248, this beast is best appreciated when the pipe is turned upside down. It's true that what matters for the smoker is the feel, balance, and functioning of a pipe. In cases like this one, the design and craftsmanship can be further enjoyed right side up, while the pipe is at rest.

*Paul Lanier sculpted
a collector's series based on
La Fontaine's Fables.*

The one on the opposite page is 8⅝ inches (22 cm) long, and this one is more than 9¾ (25 cm) inches long—not counting the stems.

While pantographic reproduction (see pages 224–225) is used in the execution of portraits on pipes, the artist's only recourse in creating these was a preliminary sketch on paper.

A Frog had an Ox in her view;
His bulk, to her, appeared ideal.
She, not even as large, all in
all, as an egg hitherto,
Envious, stretched, swelled,
strained, in her zeal
To match the beast in
overall size...

Rushing is useless; one has to leave on time. To such
Truth witness is given by the Tortoise and the Hare.
"Let's make a bet," the former once said, "that you won't touch
That line as soon as I." "As soon? Are you all there,
Neighbor?" said the rapid beast.

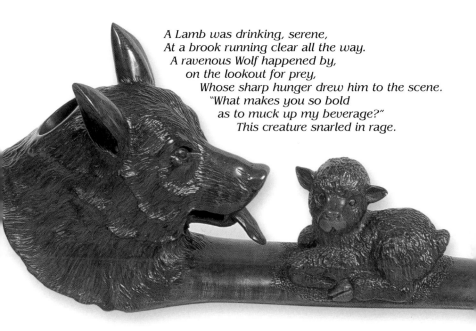

A Lamb was drinking, serene,
At a brook running clear all the way.
A ravenous Wolf happened by,
   on the lookout for prey,
      Whose sharp hunger drew him to the scene.
      "What makes you so bold
         as to muck up my beverage?"
            This creature snarled in rage.

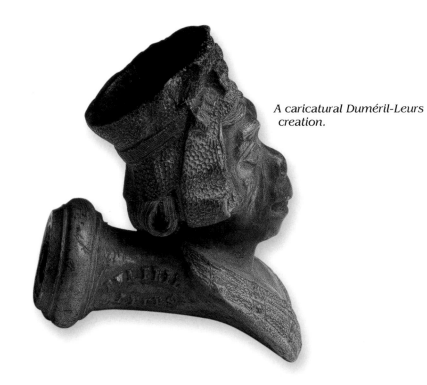

A caricatural Duméril-Leurs creation.

Griffons? Gremlins? A mix of the two?
Whatever they might be, this funny pipe
was made in Saint-Claude, France,
in the early 1900s.

These whimsical creatures have a touch of the sixteenth-century painter Pieter Bruegel in them.

As does this beggar-rat which, like the others, was made by Gambier.

IV

MEMORABLE
pipes

Once the inner architecture of pipes was pretty much standardized and the chosen materials—whether clay, meerschaum, or briarwood—were comfortably performing, decorative invention exploded. In addition to the human faces and animal races just seen, pipes appeared in the craziest and often most impractical shapes: locomotives, hats, shoes, violins, airplanes, and even tennis rackets were being lit up! And keeping up with the creative audacity of one's pipe-smoking neighbor became an art in itself.

Everyone knows that alcohol and pipe-smoking make a good match. But who would have thought of smoking from a beer stein? The white clay model is by Job-Clerc, the red by Bonnaud.

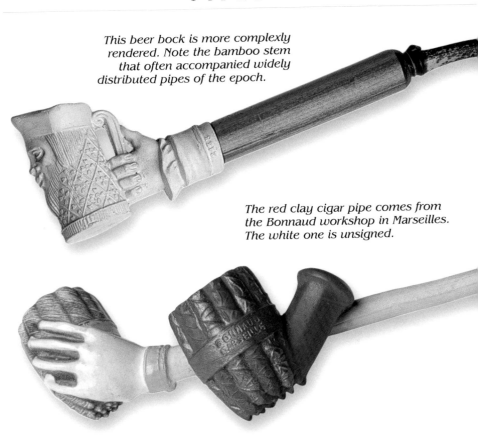

This beer bock is more complexly rendered. Note the bamboo stem that often accompanied widely distributed pipes of the epoch.

The red clay cigar pipe comes from the Bonnaud workshop in Marseilles. The white one is unsigned.

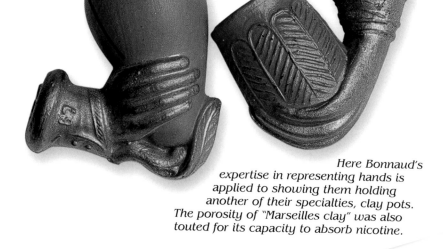

Here Bonnaud's expertise in representing hands is applied to showing them holding another of their specialties, clay pots. The porosity of "Marseilles clay" was also touted for its capacity to absorb nicotine.

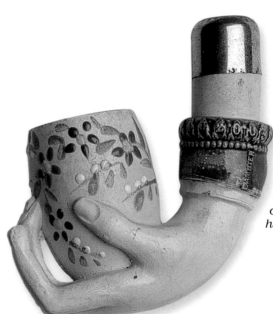

The space between the fingers and the bowl attests to the quality of this Gambier pipe. The ferrule bracelet only adds to the harmonious effect.

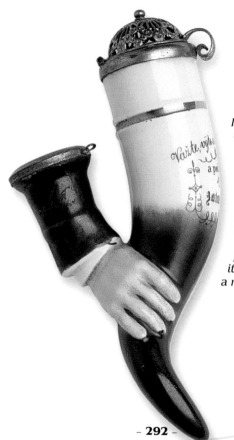

In Czechoslovakia, horn-of-plenty pipes like this one dating from the nineteenth century were often sold with commemorative inscriptions on the face. While there's nothing particularly morbid about the pipe design itself, its inscription concerns a recent death.

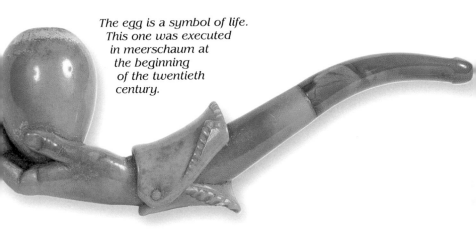

*The egg is a symbol of life.
This one was executed
in meerschaum at
the beginning
of the twentieth
century.*

Bonnaud sold these pipes to retailers in lots of twelve for a little less than a dollar a piece. Consumers must have paid two or three times as much.

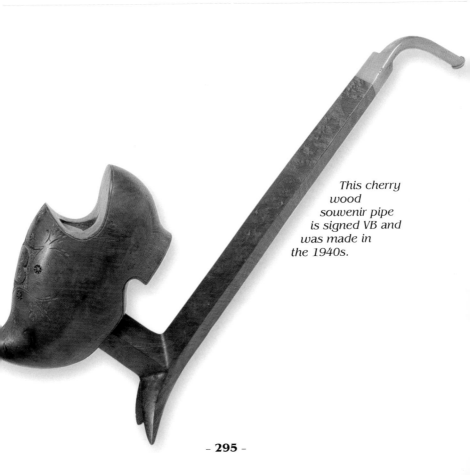

This cherry
wood
souvenir pipe
is signed VB and
was made in
the 1940s.

These two are also souvenir models, suggesting a visit to the mountains. A smoker could choose the pipe that best captured his sporting pleasure—a sturdy hiking boot …

... or a ski boot, neatly poised and ready to go on its finely curved ski.

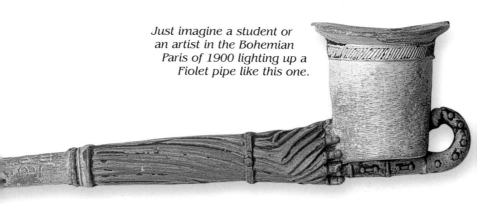

Just imagine a student or an artist in the Bohemian Paris of 1900 lighting up a Fiolet pipe like this one.

*Like those
who carved
walking stick pummels,
nutcrackers, pocket-knife
sheaths, and bottle openers,
pipe artists enjoyed using the
human leg as a model. This one
dates to the 1920s. It has a briar
bowl and an ebonite stem.*

Pipe makers were not
about to miss the train.
This locomotive was
made by Goedewaagen,
in Gouda, Holland.

Also inspired by the steam engine, the Express 3519, was created in the early twentieth century. Tobacco is packed in through the front like a coal engine. The wheels really turn, but the horizontal chamber makes it more of a collector's than a smoker's model.

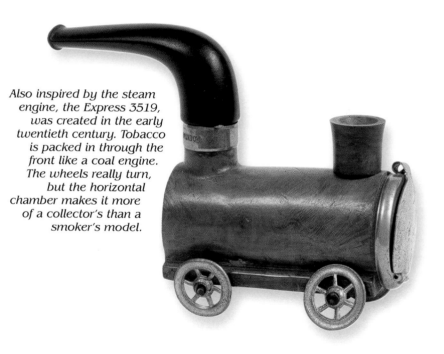

The Graf-Zeppelin flew its maiden voyage across the Atlantic in 1928. By 1932 it was making regular transatlantic crossings. It took 68 hours to fly from Europe to New York, and 89 hours in the other direction. The screw-on bowl is of briarwood, the dirigible is made of ebonite.

The first long-distance flights of the early twentieth century were met with wild enthusiasm. This pipe is among many commemorating that exciting moment.

This canon pipe, in memory of Napoleon's army, is the work of the contemporary master, Paul Lanier.

During World War I, the
"75" canon was as
famous in the French
army's artillery as canned
beef was in their rations.
This canon-shaped pipe
commemorates the fact with the
inscription "1914–1915, our 75."
It was made in Marseilles
by Bonnaud..

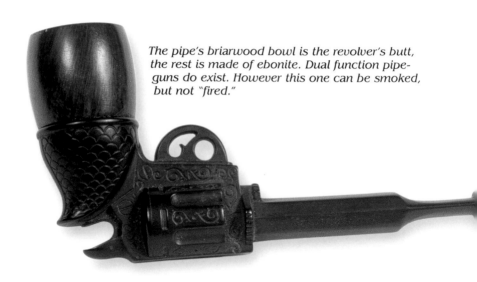

The pipe's briarwood bowl is the revolver's butt, the rest is made of ebonite. Dual function pipe-guns do exist. However this one can be smoked, but not "fired."

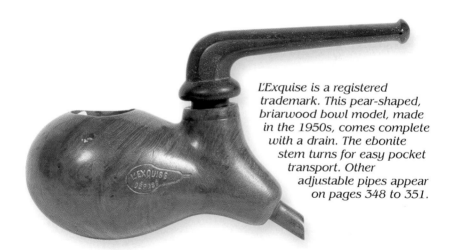

L'Exquise is a registered trademark. This pear-shaped, briarwood bowl model, made in the 1950s, comes complete with a drain. The ebonite stem turns for easy pocket transport. Other adjustable pipes appear on pages 348 to 351.

A Gambier commemorative pipe from the 1900 Paris Olympics, when tennis was already an olympic sport. Note the spigot ferrule mount.

Another tennis set. This briarwood racket-and-ball pipe dates to the 1930s and was made in Saint-Claude. Today, such a combination of sports with tobacco is nearly unthinkable.

Pipes and music go hand in hand. Here, sculptor Paul Lanier outdid himself with a phonograph pipe in which the horn serves as a bowl.

Lanier's piano pipe has a trompe-l'oeil keyboard. Both of these collector's items are made of briarwood and ebonite and date to the 1970s. For display only!

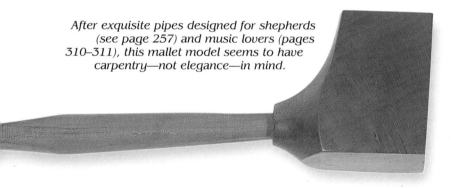

After exquisite pipes designed for shepherds (see page 257) and music lovers (pages 310–311), this mallet model seems to have carpentry—not elegance—in mind.

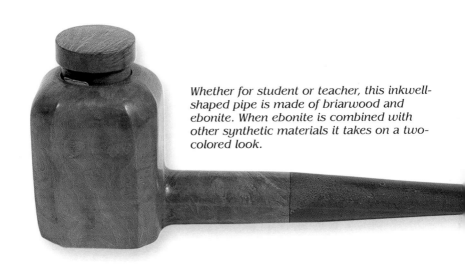

Whether for student or teacher, this inkwell-shaped pipe is made of briarwood and ebonite. When ebonite is combined with other synthetic materials it takes on a two-colored look.

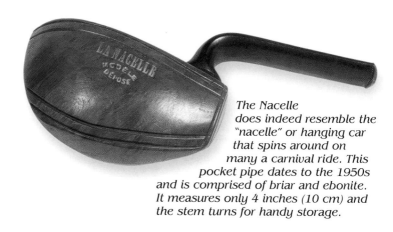

The Nacelle does indeed resemble the "nacelle" or hanging car that spins around on many a carnival ride. This pocket pipe dates to the 1950s and is comprised of briar and ebonite. It measures only 4 inches (10 cm) and the stem turns for handy storage.

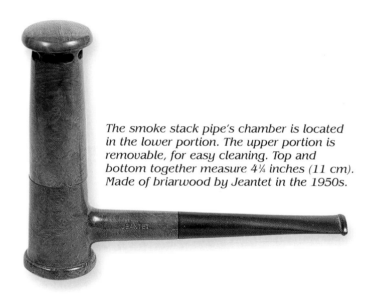

The smoke stack pipe's chamber is located in the lower portion. The upper portion is removable, for easy cleaning. Top and bottom together measure 4¼ inches (11 cm). Made of briarwood by Jeantet in the 1950s.

V

UNUSUAL
pipes

P ipe makers have always been an uncontrollably
imaginative bunch. And when such inventiveness is
matched up with skill, many a pipe dream comes
true. You are about to enter that wonder world of truly
exceptional pipes. Many of them are one-of-a-kind
masterworks. Some are homely folk-art pieces. And quite a
few are mass-produced souvenirs. But whether a graceful
goddess or a decadent death's head, they are all
curiosities, made to provoke or amaze. While you may be
content to look on and chuckle, remember that a number
of these pipes were actually puffed by smokers just dying
to be noticed.

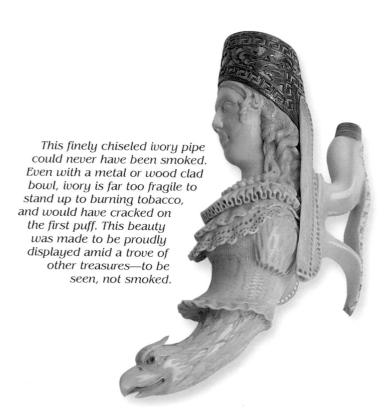

This finely chiseled ivory pipe could never have been smoked. Even with a metal or wood clad bowl, ivory is far too fragile to stand up to burning tobacco, and would have cracked on the first puff. This beauty was made to be proudly displayed amid a trove of other treasures—to be seen, not smoked.

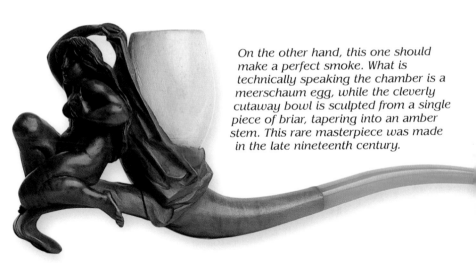

On the other hand, this one should make a perfect smoke. What is technically speaking the chamber is a meerschaum egg, while the cleverly cutaway bowl is sculpted from a single piece of briar, tapering into an amber stem. This rare masterpiece was made in the late nineteenth century.

Here is a mischievously lovely cigarette
holder that merely masquerades as a
miniature pipe. It was made before 1900,
and can be excused by the fact that
cigarette holders did not take on
their definitive long
silhouette until the 1930s.

*The imitation elephant tusk of this piece, another
antique cigarette holder, might have been a good idea.
But ivory and smoking simply don't mix. One day, the
owner must have let the cigarette burn down too far,
resulting in the disgraceful crack.*

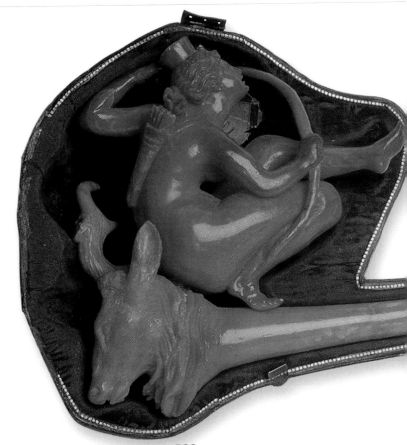

Brilliantly sculpted from two-toned amber, this marvel of a pipe depicts Diana, the Roman goddess of hunting. It was fashioned in France in the nineteenth century. The deer head and stem are carved from a single piece of amber which must have been at least a foot and a half long (45 cm), since the finished pipe is not much shorter than that. Amber has become so rare today, that such a feat is no longer possible.

Stunning agate lends a graphic flare to this squarely contoured model, with its silver lid. Too bad the stem is missing. It must have been sculpted in ivory or bone. Definitely another pipe to be seen and not smoked.

Finely worked metal is the secret to this pipe's beauty. It is of unknown origin, but probably comes from an Eastern country. Long ago metal pipes were made for European swashbucklers and swordsmen, who could stash them in their boots at the sound of enemy footsteps. For this reason, such pipes were known as musketeers.

Using nature's natural gifts is nothing new. Shells have been used for money or jewelry in many parts of the world. This nacre nautilus might easily have suggested pipe smoke to a fertile imagination. It just took a bit of clay for the chamber, a hazel wood branch for the stem, and fantasy became a reality.

*Nautilus shells served as
the foundation and inspiration
for many a lovely pipe.
The chamber was often made
of clay, in this case with
a metal rim. There are
shell pipes of all qualities,
from makeshift to
priceless masterpiece.*

These two snail shell pipes (the one on the left is of exceptional quality) come from the collection of Igor Smirnoff and Olga Boundass, siblings and Russian emigrés who settled in France.

This team, with little means but great discernment and drive, collected pipes throughout Europe, amassing a pipe trove of more than four hundred pieces.

Ghoulish and ingenious, this pipe makes use of the root's knotty surface to rise before your eyes as an apparition. The human head is mounted on a sort of toad, in turn affixed to a bird. A larger, bear-like animal is at the bottom of the heap.

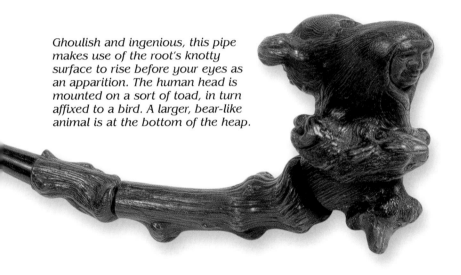

No less disquieting is this image of hell by Duméril-Leurs. The female figures float in their flames of suffering. Just imagine the effect of red embers glowing out from the bowl.

It would seem daring indeed to make a pipe in the shape of Death today. More than a century ago, Gambier was apparently not afraid of such associations.

There was a vogue for death's-head pipes among nineteenth-century Parisian students. The well-seasoned white clay pipe is a Gambier, the red is a Bonnaud.

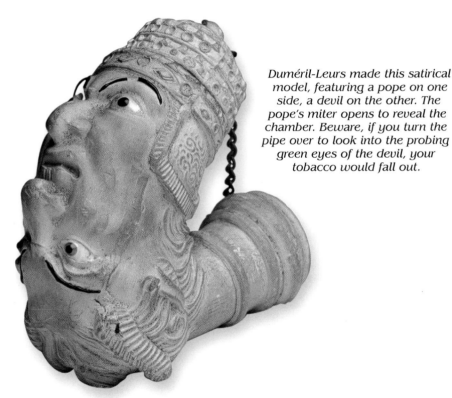

Duméril-Leurs made this satirical model, featuring a pope on one side, a devil on the other. The pope's miter opens to reveal the chamber. Beware, if you turn the pipe over to look into the probing green eyes of the devil, your tobacco would fall out.

In this case as the pipe smoker converses, his or her friend can enjoy the calm view of a roosting bird. When sitting in a pipe rack it's the more or less crabby-faced man that one sees; briar and ebonite, 1920s.

Does this double-faced creature say something about its owner? The pipe presents two moods: the serious (verging on mean) and the carefree (even clownish).

This colorful wonder was made by Gambier in the nineteenth century. It represents a boisterous student at France's Saint-Cyr Military Academy, an establishment that was known for rowdiness.

GAMBIER.

The Picard company of Rennes, France made this clay commemorative pipe in honor of Napoloeon III's visit to the ports of Cherbourg and Brest in 1858.

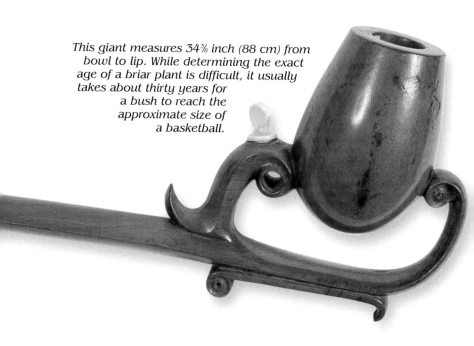

This giant measures 34⅜ inch (88 cm) from bowl to lip. While determining the exact age of a briar plant is difficult, it usually takes about thirty years for a bush to reach the approximate size of a basketball.

On the other hand, this one measures a more manageable 11 inches (28 cm). Both date from the first half of the twentieth century. Note the blond horn stem and the valve. Such a valve is necessary when the air hole passage is curved.

The bowl is a classic Belgian model, but the stem is quite unusual, at just under a foot (30 cm) long! Just imagine the skill required of its nineteenth-century creator in the making of an air hole passage—which is square-shaped the entire way through.

More proof that a pipe's
originality may lie in its
stem rather than its bowl; this
one measures 15¾ inches (40 cm)
and is made of painted wood. Here
too, the air hole remains rectilinear the
whole way through.

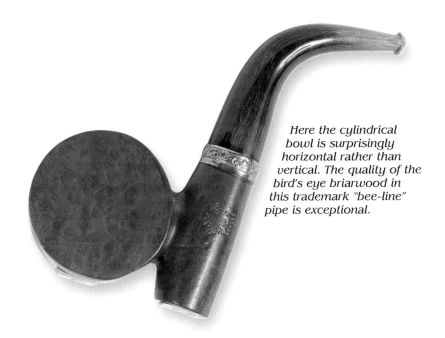

Here the cylindrical bowl is surprisingly horizontal rather than vertical. The quality of the bird's eye briarwood in this trademark "bee-line" pipe is exceptional.

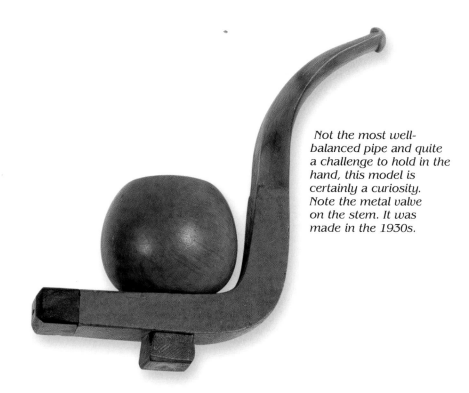

Not the most well-balanced pipe and quite a challenge to hold in the hand, this model is certainly a curiosity. Note the metal valve on the stem. It was made in the 1930s.

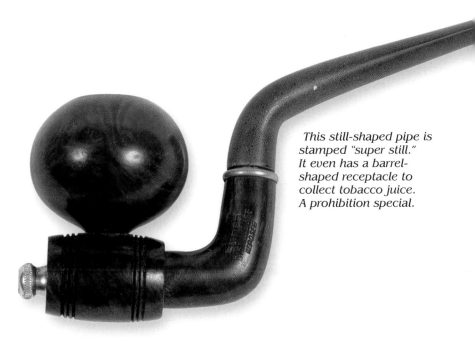

This still-shaped pipe is stamped "super still." It even has a barrel-shaped receptacle to collect tobacco juice. A prohibition special.

Although they sometimes seem like strange contraptions, foldable pipes are practical and smoke just fine. This one is made of sandblasted and dyed briarwood and has an ebonite stem. All three of these pipes were made in the 1950s. Adjustable stems enable one to gain about an inch and a half (3 to 4 cm).

*Sometimes, after long and faithful use, the joints of
folding pipes such as these become loose and are
liable to start swiveling in the middle of a smoke*

This can be very amusing—or quite dangerous.
These two models are made of briarwood and
date from the 1950s.

The realm of tobacco seems to invite exotic appellations, whether or not they have anything to do with the object being named. The Persanne is a case in point. There is nothing Persian about it, in fact it was made in good old Saint-Claude. Still its interesting patch-work is a bit more refined than that on the facing page.

It was once said of the popular French cartoonist, Albert Dubout, that God would be shocked by his drawings. It's true that he drew every pair of pants with a patch, every shoe with a hole, and every pipe as a makeshift piece. The above briarwood (and wire) pipe, from the 1950s, was directly inspired by Dubout's cartoons.

Tourists flocked to the small village of Barbizon, at the edge of the Fontainebleau Forest in the mid-nineteenth-century when many painters including Camille Corot and Gustave Courbet had studios there. Among the souvenirs brought home were pipes that functioned like this one.

Our model, made in Saint-Claude in the late nineteenth century, is of higher quality than those sold as Barbizon souvenirs. The body of this severe-looking judge harbors a pipe stem while his right hand grasps a cigarette holder.

All known walking-stick pipes are handmade, and therefore one of a kind. When the pipe is disassembled the bowl serves as the stick's grip and the other parts fit securely within. The stem can also be used as a cigarette holder.

This model is more unusual. The entire walking stick serves as a pipe. One might consider a pipe like this impractical, but the seasoning proves that it was actually used. The bullet cartridge has been modified for tobacco tamping.

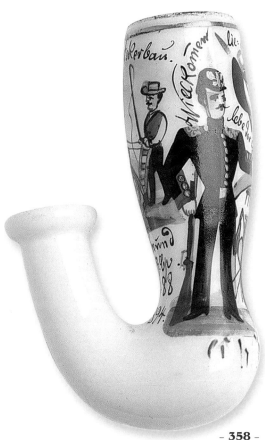

Porcelain pipes often told their owner's life story. This one, which is exceptional both for the conception and the rendering of its design, tells the story of a recruit's discharge from the French army in 1888. Such pipes are sometimes more amusing than actual comic strips.

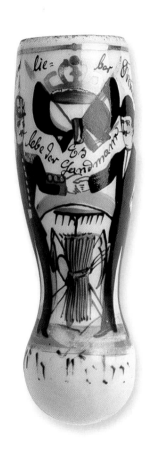

While in the seventeenth century, pipe bowls were usually quite small, reflecting the price of tobacco at the time, this hefty Bacchus would have swallowed up a whole package in one shot. The exceptional porcelain table pipe was probably made in Andenne, Belgium. The stem would have been flexible, similar to that of a hookah.

In nineteenth-century Germany, pipes, such as this porcelain drunk with a beer keg, had all sorts of inscriptions depending on the client's taste. The only common denominator seems to have been a not very veiled allusion to drinking.

This folding pipe is a prototype
designed by François Achilli for
Butz-Choquin. The bowl is in
briarwood and the stem, if the
term even applies here,
is made of a
synthetic plastic.

If you are hoping to buy one of these highly
stylized pipes the sad news is that they are
both one-of-a-kind research prototypes. They
may one day be placed on a crowded shelf of
some pipe collector who will judge them as
being either great advances or crazy ideas

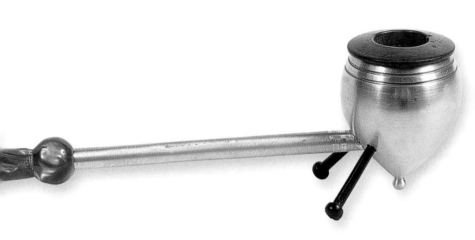

*Like all industrial design creations, such
questions are often a matter of personal taste.
In any event, the perfect pipe that is as simple
and handy to smoke as a cigarette, and free
from bothersome ceremonial trappings, is still
waiting to be invented.*

Index, Addresses & Bibliography

Index

The index includes the major brands, manufacturers, and place-names
mentioned in the book, as well as the names, characters, objects,
and themes represented.

INDEX

INDEX

INDEX

Acknowledgments

WIth special thanks to Philippe Séverin for his friendship and his expertise in clay pipes; Daniel Mazaleyrat for permitting us to photograph some of his rare pieces; Christine Grenard, Secretary of the Confrérie des maîtres-pipiers de Saint-Claude; Joël Bride of the Musée de la Pipe et du Diamant for his accessibility and assistance; Alain Tribondeau and Mme Bouchenter of the Musée d'art et d'histoire Marcel Dessal.

Thanks also to Guy Devautour and Clare Ducamp.

Addresses

FRANCE
Confrérie des maîtres-pipiers de Saint-Claude
45, rue du Pré – B.P. 32, 39201 Saint-Claude
tel. and fax: 03 84 45 04 02 · confreri@club-internet.fr

Musée d'art et d'histoire Marcel Dessai
7, Place du Musée, 28100 Dreux
tel: 02 37 50 18 61 · fax: 02 37 38 84 13

Musée de la Pipe et du Diamant
1, place Jacques-Faizant, 39200 Saint-Claude
tel: 03 84 45 17 00 · fax: 03 84 45 18 97

GERMANY
Tabakhistorische Sammlung Reemtsma
22605, Parkstrasse 51, Hamburg
tel: 82 20 19 58

HOLLAND
De Moriaan Museum
Westhaven 29, 2801 PB Gouda
tel: 01820 88444

Pipenkabinet
Prinsengracht 488, 1017 Amsterdam
tel: 020 4211779

ITALY
Museo della Pipa
Gavirate (Varese), Via del Chiostro
tel: 0332/743334
www.hcs.it/varese/aptv/museo_della_pips.htm

SCOTLAND
Huntley House Museum
142 Canongate, Edinburgh EH8 8DD
tel: 031 225 2424

UNITED KINGDOM
Broseley Pipeworks
Ironbridge Gorge Museum, Telford, Shropshire, TF8 7AW
tel: 44 0 1952 432 166 · fax: 44 0 1952 432 204
visits@ironbridge.org.uk · www.ironbridge.org.uk

Pitt-Rivers Museum
South Parks Road, Oxford OX1 3PP
Tel: 01865 270927

UNITED STATES
The George Arents Tobacco Collection
The New York Public Library, Room 324/8
Fifth Avenue and 42nd Street, New York 10018-2788
tel: 212 930 0801 · fax: 212 302 4815
arnref@nypl.org · www.nypl.org/research/chss/spe/rbk/arents.html

Museum of Tobacco Art and History
8th Avenue and Harrison Street, Nashville, TN
Tel: 615 880 4500
www.artcom.com/Museums/vs/mr/37203.htm

SELECTED INTERNET SITES
www.greenforest.com/127/
www.keepsmilin.com/meerschaum.html
www.naspc.org · www.pipeguy.com · www.pipecollectors.org
www.scpr.fsnet.co.uk/pages/homepage.htm

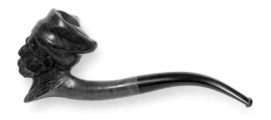

Bibliography

Crole, Robin. *Pipe, the Art and Lore of a Great Tradition.*
Roseville, Calif.: Prima Publishing, 1999.

Hacker, Richard Carleton. Rare Smoke, *The Ultimate Guide to Pipe Collecting.*
Beverly Hills: Autumngold Publishers, 1989.

Hacker, Richard Carleton. *The Ultimate Pipe Book.*
London: Souvenir Press, 1989.

Liebaert, Alexis, and Alan Maya, with Jacques P. Cole.
The Illustrated History of the Pipe.
London: Harold Starck Publishers, Ltd., 1994.

Rapaport, Ben. *Collecting Antique Meerschaum Pipes.*
Atgen, Penn.: Schiffer Publishing, 1999.

Rapaport, Ben, et al. *A Complete Guide to Collecting Antique Pipes.*
Atgen, Penn.: Schiffer Publishing, 1998.

Wright, David. *The Pipe Companion: A Connoisseur's Guide.*
Philadelphia: Running Press Companion, 2000.

In the same collection

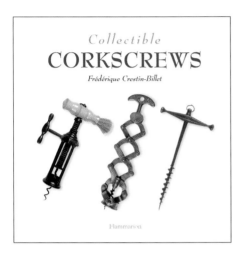

Collectible CORKSCREWS
Frédérique Crestin-Billet

Collectible POCKET KNIVES
Dominique Pascal

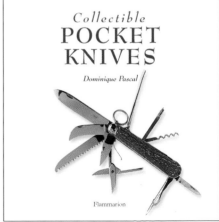

Collectible MINIATURE
PERFUME BOTTLES
Anne Breton

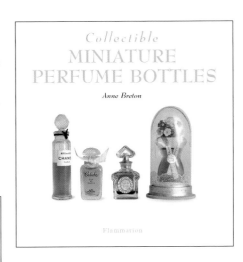

Collectible MINIATURE CARS
Dominique Pascal

Collectible FOUNTAIN PENS
J. M. Clark

Collectible WRISTWATCHES
René Pannier

Collectible SNOWDOMES
Lélie Carnot

Collectible
SNOWDOMES

Lélie Carnot

Flammarion

Photographic credits

Text credits

FA0884-02-VI
Dépot légal: 06/2002